About Demos

Demos is a greenhouse for new ideas which can improve the quality of our lives. As an independent think tank, we aim to create an open resource of knowledge and learning that operates beyond traditional party politics.

We connect researchers, thinkers and practitioners to an international network of people changing politics. Our ideas regularly influence government policy, but we also work with companies, NGOs, colleges and professional bodies.

Demos knowledge is organised around five themes, which combine to create new perspectives. The themes are democracy, learning, enterprise, quality of life and global change.

But we also understand that thinking by itself is not enough. Demos has helped to initiate a number of practical projects which are delivering real social benefit through the redesign of public services.

For Demos, the process is as important as the final product. We bring together people from a wide range of backgrounds to cross-fertilise ideas and experience. By working with Demos, our partners help us to develop sharper insight into the way ideas shape society.

www.demos.co.uk

First published in 2003

ISBN 1 84180 110 0
Typeset by Land & Unwin, Bugbrooke
Printed by Printflow, London

For further information and
subscription details please contact:

Demos
The Mezzanine
Elizabeth House
39 York Road
London SE1 7NQ

telephone: 020 7401 5330
email: mail@demos.co.uk
web: www.demos.co.uk

The Risk Factor

Making the child protection system work for children

Andrew Cooper
Rachael Hetherington
Ilan Katz

DEMOS

Contents

Acknowledgements

This book is the result of many years of collaborative work with a wide range of people without whose creativity and dedication to helping children at risk we would not have developed these ideas or committed them to paper.

We would like to thank colleagues who were involved in the series of cross-national research programmes and seminars we undertook through the 1990s. These provided the basic insights that there are other ways of doing things, and that we can change our basic assumptions about how to help children and families.

Colleagues in our 'home' institutions – Brunel University, the Tavistock Centre, the University of East London, NSPCC and the Children and Young People's Unit – have supported us over the years in developing these ideas.

The staff at Demos have also been helpful and supportive and we are fortunate in Demos' willingness to take this project forward. A lively seminar convened by Demos to discuss a draft of the book was very useful, and thanks to all who participated.

Our family and friends have encouraged us and put up with long meetings and phonecalls, and we would like to acknowledge their patience and consideration.

Andrew Cooper, Rachael Hetherington and Ilan Katz
June 2003

1. Introduction

Child protection and welfare systems need reform. This is apparent at a number of different levels: the Laming Inquiry into the death of Victoria Climbié; the negative media portrayal of child protection work; public mistrust of child welfare professionals; limited improvements in outcomes for children; and the recruitment and retention crisis in the social work profession.

But structural change is pointless without reshaping the relationship between the child, the family and the state at a more fundamental level. This relationship is played out every day in meetings between families, social workers and other professionals. Without an adequate understanding of the *culture* of this system, further reform will be unsustainable and possibly counterproductive.

This pamphlet uses systems theory to help clarify how cultural factors such as behavioural and professional norms, value systems, and emotional and psychological states which are at the heart of child protection must be addressed. Systems thinking helps us understand why it is that organisational cultures can survive successive structural reforms, but also how they can be vulnerable to gradual erosion of trust and morale.

The child protection system can and should change to reflect changes in society. We are now less tolerant of risk. There is more poverty among young families than a generation ago. There is more available evidence and information about the successes and failures of child protection work – particularly from the perspective of children. Government is investing more in preventative work and the notion of child protection is expanding into a broader view of child welfare.

These shifts in thinking are important, but reform will only succeed if the cultural factors that characterise the relationship between the child, the family and the state are kept firmly in mind. An understanding of how positively to influence cultural factors becomes ever more critical as the government promotes preventative work and multiagency practice involving vastly different professions such as education, medicine and childcare. New ideas are therefore essential.

Is there a perfect system?

Not everyone agrees that the child protection system needs to change. According to some knowledgeable commentators, England has the best system of child protection in the world. Many others hold it to be in deep crisis. In the face of such wildly conflicting evaluations, the reasonable person might ask to see some evidence for these judgements in order to decide which view is right.

But it turns out that this helps only a little, because while there is a plethora of apparently good recent research studies in this field, they also conflict and often appear to ask and answer different and incompatible questions. Evidence-based practice and policy turn out to be more complex than they first appeared. What, then, is going on and how should we proceed?

Part of the reason for these contradictions is that the child protection system is judged against a yardstick of changing cultural values. So, for example, there is much more public awareness of child abuse. While this has had its drawbacks, such as the moral panics fuelled by tabloid newspapers, the fact that children and the pain they suffer are being taken seriously is a genuine step forward.

However, it is also true that fear of failure has shaped child protection practice in England and Wales for several decades. A non-accidental child death is a classic instance of a low probability/high consequence risk that leads to risk-averse cultures and practices in all walks of life.

The risks apply to practioners involved in child protection work as well as to children. The fear of public inquiries hangs over professionals if things go wrong. The system encourages social workers to protect their own position, in a way which runs counter to the lessons and principles they learned during their training.

But even though cultural values are integral to the operation as well as the interpretation of our child protection system, an adequate understanding of their impact has been missing from the last phase of reform. Our concern is that it will also be absent from the next.

The Victoria Climbié inquiry report describes a catalogue of errors and failures. We see how people repeatedly failed to come to grips professionally with the evidence that was presented to them. The report responds by suggesting a further tightening of rules and procedures and some structural changes to the delivery of services. While the structural changes recommended may bring some improvements, they do not face the underlying problems. Change to organisational structures without change in the underlying organisational culture has failed in the past and is unlikely to succeed now.

The Department of Health's recently published *Framework for the Assessment of Children in Need and their Families* is welcome, but the 10-year record on improvements in child outcomes is poor. Although the prevalence of child abuse itself remains extremely hard to calculate, there appears to be a huge gap between the numbers of children who have contact with the child protection system, and the actual numbers of children being abused.[1]

The forthcoming Cabinet Office green paper on children at risk is likely to recommend more multiagency working aimed at prevention, as well as improved child protection procedures. While these moves are potentially very positive, there is a real danger that they will underplay issues of cultural differences that exist between different kinds of professionals.

There is no perfect child protection system. Child protection systems have to respond to a wide range of different situations, different not only in severity, but also in kind. These include, for example, children being left by parents while they go to the pub, over chastisement, becoming involved in internet pornography, being sexually harassed by a classmate, children sexually abused by residential workers, babies being shaken by child minders and so on.

Most previous reforms of the system have had a specific case or type of case in mind. Invariably this has resulted in losers as well as winners. In such a complex situation it is inevitable that there will be unintended consequences. What is required is a combination of respect for the inevitability of complexity, allied to purposeful work in the interests of children, and continual attention to questions of rights and justice. We argue that systems theory is the best foundation from which to conceptualise and mobilise change.

Understanding systems

The main theoretical basis for our argument is provided by complex, or open, systems theory, and by the ecological model. This approach is becoming increasingly important in contemporary understandings of policy and practice in human services. According to this analysis, social systems are not driven by equilibrium but rather by complex and constant change.

Interventions at any point in the system will create consequences, but these are not easily predictable from the initial parameters of the system, and are not necessarily proportionate to the input itself. At a psychological level, this means living with uncertainty and accepting that uncertainty is fundamental to policy management and practice in child welfare.

The apparent inability of government to think in terms of systems instead of structures, and cultures instead of procedures, is extremely damaging and has contributed to the apparent malfunctioning of crucial parts of the system:

- The nature of the system does not encourage anyone – children, parents or the public – to report child abuse, so many children are not protected.

- The procedures are ineffective in sorting out the serious situations from those which do not need to give rise to such a high level of concern.
- The system as a whole is highly bureaucratic and inflexible.
- The decision-making of professionals in child protection is dominated by the need to comply with rules and procedures.
- Children find the system traumatic – sometimes more traumatic than the abuse itself.

The Government is interested in creating an IT system which could track individual children, collate risk factors and trigger professional action. Several information, referral and tracking (IRT) pilots are already running and this approach underpinned government thinking which fed into the children at risk green paper.

Information sharing is important and databases should be a part of any attempt to store and analyse data. However, the real risk assessment must be done by child professionals who base their judgments on daily interactions with children and families. The danger is that over-reliance on automated risk assessment systems will actually reduce the capacity of child protection practitioners to identify and manage the risks to children.

New principles: trust, authority and negotiation

Systems thinking tells us that cultural systems cannot be controlled, but this does not mean that systems cannot be effectively managed. In fact, our analysis shows that the basis of the system should be trust, and that trust can inform effective relationship-based practice in child protection work. But we have lost trust in trust for a number of reasons:

- a change in public attitudes, which means that people are less ready to accept official opinion
- a general attack, often backed by the media, on the professions as a reliable source of knowledge and expertise

- a lack of resources for professionals to offer to families in need
- a lack of time for the professionals to establish trust;
- a managerial tendency which favours short-term solutions
- The bureaucracy and inflexibility of the system; once the child protection process is initiated it generates its own momentum.

Trust should be the fundamental principle underpinning a reformed system. The others should be authority and negotiation.

By authority we mean the ability of the relevant professionals to work with confidence in their own knowledge and understanding, and confidence in the support of both their management and the wider community for their values. Without the flexibility and confidence of this kind of authority, interventions are tentative, bureaucratic and proceduralised.

Negotiation is more than a one-off process to solve a specific problem. It is an approach that emphasises dialogue and discussion, even in difficult circumstances. In most child welfare conflicts there is room for negotiation over some aspects of the situation, and the process of negotiation may open up new possibilities arising from greater knowledge and understanding.

These are systemic principles that describe how social systems can operate most effectively in dealing with conflict. In the later chapters of the pamphlet we describe in more detail a number of changes that could be made now, almost regardless of structures that emerge from the next round of reform.

Applying the principles

Establishing trust, authority or negotiation cannot be done by edict.

Small-scale experimentation is encouraging and could lead, by example, a major culture change in the child protection system. An innovative project in Nottingham has established a number of changes based upon the three principles we describe.

These include a more structured use of 'Child in Need' assessments, a professional forum where social workers can discuss complex cases, and a negotiation meeting staffed by trained mediators. These have had the effect of lowering the ante and reducing the high numbers of children caught up in the system.

There is sustained pressure on policy-makers to introduce more procedures to reduce risk; it is very hard to swim against that tide. However, systems thinking shows us that models designed for risk management in other areas of professional life such as accountancy, car manufacture or pollution control, have been misapplied to child protection work.

There are both explicit and implicit risks: risks of intervention (trauma for children); risks of non-intervention (continued abuse); risks to third parties (siblings, neighbours); and risks to professionals (getting it wrong, stepping over organisational boundaries, misusing scarce resources). Our argument is that *trust*, rather than control, management or elimination, is the surest foundation for achieving risk reduction.

Of course, in an emergency children will be removed from families. In some cases children need to be removed earlier and more decisively than at present. But projects like the one in Nottingham, examined later in this report, show how respite from formal procedures can be built into the system. Extended across the country, this would reduce the tendency for child protection cases to career towards an unnecessary rescue or a day in court.

The runaway nature of the risk driven system is compounded by a growing confidentiality crisis. On the one hand, confidentiality is deemed to be a fundamental part of the professional/client relationship and is essential if this relationship is to be built on trust. On the other, hand child welfare and child protection require information to be shared between professionals, and this cannot always be done with consent.

We do not propose a principle of absolute confidentiality. But we think that there should be a period of negotiation where children and/or their parents can explore their complex dilemmas, and receive counselling and support for a limited time. In Nottingham, a negotiation meeting has fulfilled this role and we recommend forums like this should be used more widely.

Key recommendations

Other recommendations which would work towards implementing some of the principles of trust, authority and negotiation would be:

- a greater use of 'confidential spaces' where child welfare concerns can be discussed by anybody within designated boundaries
- a relocation of more social workers from town halls to multidisciplinary teams based in schools, health centres and the community
- non-managerial supervision of social workers
- more autonomy for individual social workers within a team so that they are given responsibility for their own work in a similar way to GPs
- the introduction of negotiation forums as part of child protection proceedings; trained mediators should be part of these forums as well as a part of the overall system
- changes in Area Child Protection Committees to allow more community involvement and the introduction of statutory powers.

Child protection is perhaps the most demanding, conflict-ridden, worrying and controversial of modern public services. That is because in exercising its responsibilities to safeguard children, the state uses its power to become involved in the most intimate and sensitive family relationships.

The public is frightened of the system that has been set up to protect their children. If we can think through the principles that create the structures for its provision, then we are likely to have a model which can be adapted to inform the way other public services could operate. This is a major challenge, but it is what thinking about the future of public services must face up to.

2. A system in need of reform

Since a series of child deaths and subsequent inquiries in the early 1980s there has been a great deal of concern about the nature of child protection and child welfare services. Despite occasional attempts by government and the Association of Directors of Social Services (ADSS) among others, to portray our child protection system as working well, there is evidence that our system is neither effective at protecting children nor protecting their families.

There have been a number of positive developments in child protection over the last ten years, with both practice and policy moving on in a number of important ways.

The recognition that parents, and more recently children, should be considered as participants or partners in the child protection process has been a very significant development. In particular it is now accepted that parents, and at least some children, should be permitted to attend meetings, contribute to decisions about their lives, and express their views about the process.

Another significant development has been the increase in awareness of child abuse among the general population. While this has also had its drawbacks, most notably the moral panics created from time to time by tabloid newspapers, the fact that children and the pain they can suffer are being taken seriously is a genuine step forward. Children are now also far better protected from sexual offenders who target them in schools and residential units; convicted sex offenders are now more tightly monitored.

The Department of Health (DoH) has published a clear and well-evidenced model for the process of making assessments on child protection, the *Framework for the Assessment of Children in Need and their Families*.[2] Its implementation is another largely positive development because it attempts to institutionalise a psychosocial model for thinking about child and family problems, and has the potential to raise the standard of assessment throughout the country.

In recent years there has been a significant investment by government in children and families, and in particular into preventive programmes. Annex 1 lists some of the policies and initiatives aimed at improving the lives of socially excluded children and young people and their families. This is an impressive record, and although there has been some concern about the sheer number of initiatives, and their sometimes overlapping objectives, the overall picture of preventive services has improved considerably since the present government came to power.

Nevertheless, the overall trend in the mainstream child welfare system, especially the child protection system, has not been positive. There is no real indication that the quality of the day-to-day services being offered to children and families are better than ten years ago, or that outcomes for children and families have improved.

Part of the problem is the breakdown of faith in public services as a whole. The child protection system is probably the least well regarded and most criticised aspect of public welfare provision. Not only has it been lambasted by the media, it has been attacked by politicians, service users and the professionals themselves. The setting up of the Laming Inquiry into the death of Victoria Climbié, the eight-year old girl who died from neglect at the hands of her great aunt and her great aunt's boyfriend, was an admission that in child protection there is a real problem. The findings of the Inquiry confirmed deep-seated difficulties in processes for protecting children.

But beyond the problems stemming from lack of public confidence and media criticism, there are particular problems inherent in the current system. Three frequently identified problems are the system's lack of child focus, the failure of professionals to efficiently assess cases and communicate adequately about them with each other, and the system's potential to further traumatise those involved.

Although children have an important perspective to offer, their voices can often be lost in the decision-making forums of the child protection system. Most activity and thought is focused on the adults rather than the child.[3]

Only a small proportion of the children who are abused are ever reported to statutory child protection agencies. Those referrals by children themselves form an even smaller number. Even when the cases are reported to agencies, their filtering can be inefficient, with some situations being inappropriately treated as child protection, while serious cases are underplayed or missed.

Many children and adult survivors who have reported abuse to the authorities are critical of the help they received, and a high proportion regret ever having disclosed abuse. In the same way, children and families drawn into the child protection process frequently find the whole experience traumatic, and sometimes more traumatic than the abuse itself.

For example, procedures of child protection conferences and the child protection register are very formal, and even professionals find them intimidating. Both parents and professionals know that the child protection conference may be the only way of unlocking resources, but its human cost is to be caught up in an unstoppable process that has the potential to lead to family break-up. Parents dislike and fear child protection conferences even when the process has resulted in some practical help or emotional support being made available.

Legal intervention of any sort also produces trauma, giving little incentive for children to disclose abuse, or for parents who are worried about their own parenting to come forward for help.

Professional practice in crisis

There is a recruitment crisis in social and child welfare work. Despite government-led initiatives such as *Quality Protects* and *Sure Start*, the system has constantly fewer resources for mainstream day-to-day

The effect of child abuse

How might a system prevent the following?

Recently the press carried the account of a count hearing, concerning a 12-year-old boy convicted of taking part in a vigilante killing. The boy, who was eleven at the time, alleged that the man had indecently assaulted him. He went with his elder brother and friend to the man's house. The boy hit the alleged perpetrator in the testicles and the friend stabbed the man to death.

In court his counsel argued that a custodial sentence would be counterproductive. 'The things that he has seen and endured are extreme. He is the victim of long-standing neglect and harsh physical abuse at home. There is an explicit history of harsh physical violence at home. He has been hit until he wets himself, and appeared dirty and unkempt at school. He has been consigned to chaos through no fault of his own and now bears the consequences.'

'We know how he will behave in a secure unit with other disturbed children. He will do what he has been doing since he was six, which is to seek to stand up for himself and make a place for himself at the top of the pecking order. It's what he always does to survive.'

Guardian, 27 July 2002

work with children and families. Potential workers now see demoralised and burnt-out staff, weighed down by bureaucracy and lacking managerial support. In comparative research studies of social workers across Europe, the morale of English social workers, compared with their colleagues in other countries, was particularly low; they felt unsupported by the system.

Child protection professionals in general, and social workers in particular, are caught between the knowledge that their safest course is to propel families into the child protection system, and at the same time that the experience will very likely be negative for the family, and that the process is very difficult to reverse.

Although there are constant injunctions towards more joined-up working, interagency relationships have deteriorated due to constant changes of structure, staff shortages and agencies focusing on core business or targets. Despite the importance of family support and prevention, most resources are still focused on high-risk situations and crises. The thresholds for intervention, if anything, are being raised.

New legislation and government guidance, while genuinely aimed at making the process fairer and more transparent, has also made the work more complex and conflicted. For example, the Human Rights Act and requirements over data protection have both served to polarise 'child protection' cases from 'family support' cases, while government guidance calls for a reduction of the differentiation between the two.

These problems have been recognised by policy-makers, and their proposed solution has been to expand managerialism. There has been an explosion of government guidance, advice and targets from the centre. In the 1980s there was virtually no central government oversight of child welfare practice. By the end of the 1990s there was a plethora of guidelines, strategies, targets and league tables. Today a quality industry structure has been constructed by central government to govern it all, consisting of the Audit Commission, the Social Services Inspectorate, the Social Care Institute for Excellence, the General Social Care Council and the Care Standards Commission.

There is a sense that these increasingly frenetic developments really amount to a shifting around of the deckchairs on the Titanic. We have travelled as far down the managerialist route as is possible, and yet the fundamental problems still remain. On this analysis, the problem is not about professional practice becoming more 'child-focused', 'joined-up', 'evidence-based' or 'high quality'. Failures to communicate are the symptoms, not causes, of the difficulties that the system experiences.

The underlying problem is the fundamental relationship between children, families and the state. Professional practice is only one factor in this relationship, and all these new developments are, in the end, merely bureaucratic responses to what is really a problem of civil society.

Weighing the pig – the problem of contemporary welfare culture

We are arguing for a change to the whole child protection system of England and Wales, so we cannot avoid engaging with the context in which the child protection system functions. Comparative research into different systems of child protection shows that they are powerfully shaped by the history, politics, and legal cultures of the nation state in which they evolved.[4]

In England and Wales the child protection system is culturally and historically shaped by several different but interrelated factors. The most important of these are:

- our adversarial legal system and the strong emphasis in our legal culture on individual rights
- our idea of the welfare state, and the state in general, as something residual which is only called on to intervene in private or civil life when things go wrong, or when there is a clear structural deficit in social provision. To be a citizen does not entail feeling or believing that you are part of, or have any obligations towards the state. Participation is something which 'it' calls on 'us' to engage in, or 'we' demand of 'it'. Other countries, including to some extent Scotland, think of the relationship between the citizen (and therefore the child in the family) and the state more inclusively and holistically
- the dissolution, weakening or individualising over recent decades of many of the layers of intermediate institutions in public life (trade unions, community associations, professional associations, friendly societies) which once organised and mediated civil society in its relationship to the individual, the family and the state. This has affected the nature of the institutions of child welfare and protection, which have themselves at the same time become over-legalised or proceduralised
- the extremely troubled and controversial history of child

protection services since at least 1984; the culture of public enquiries into child deaths and abuse scandals, allied to media outrage and the vilification of professionals, has put the entire system on the defensive and sapped the confidence of those working within it

- the widespread growth of a culture of risk-aversion in the welfare state and society at large; that has resulted in an institutionalised social preoccupation with performance monitoring, quality assurance and the centralised policy control of professional standards and behaviour. As one observer commented, we are spending so much time weighing the pig we have forgotten to feed it.

All of these factors, working in complex interactions, often outside the control of policy-makers, have resulted in a tendency to resort to law and procedures in child protection matters rather than mediation, negotiation or professional judgement. They have also led to the establishment of quasi-judicial institutions in child protection work such as the child protection register and the child protection conference.

Both have generated a system relatively closed to the possibility of relationship-based practice and institutional management in which negotiation, mediation, and personal judgement are fundamental. These are the forms of practice and organisational functioning which we are arguing should be reinvigorated and revalidated.

Cases too horrific to face

Nowhere is the failure to attend to the importance of relationships in modern child welfare work more clearly revealed than in the Inqury report into the death of Victoria Climbié.

We would argue that the problems with relationships, highlighted in the report, are a central feature of all failures in child protection work: working relationships are placed under extreme (and often insidious) pressure by the very extremity of what is happening in serious child abuse cases, and the system either fails to pick this up, or

Keeping the child in mind

In spite of the emphasis on the welfare of the child that is explicit in the Children Act 1989, the views of children are often ignored in the process of protecting them. In struggling families, parents often have major problems in their own right and when that happens, it is hard for professionals not to lose sight of the child.

For example, Hetherington et al (2001) found that if a parent has a mental health problem, virtually all the professional attention tends to be focused on this issue rather than on the needs or perspectives of the children. Some other European countries make more explicit provision for the voice of the child. We have no equivalent to the statement in the German Children Act, the *Kinder und Jugendhilfegesitz* 1990, that 'Children and young people can be counselled without the knowledge of the legal parent or guardian if the counselling is necessary due to need or conflict of interest and as long as the aim of the counselling is undermined if the parent or guardian is informed'.[5]

itself mirror the same pressures.

As Lord Laming said in his report, Victoria Climbié might have been saved had people 'done straightforward things well'. But there is little or nothing in the report to help us understand why people did not do these things. It begins with an impassioned and wide-ranging series of reflections, analyses, and judgements, but it ends much as most inquiry reports have, by resort to a combination of recommendations for structural change and tightening of procedures. In between are the lengthy narrative reconstructions of contact between the various services, Victoria herself, and those who were supposed to be caring for her. Through these stories we see that people repeatedly failed to come to grips professionally with the evidence that was presented to them. But we do not see why and how this happened.

The evidence for Victoria's condition was staring people in the face. Some appear to have understood and recorded what they believed was probably happening to her, and some did not. Where they did, people either did not follow through on their assessments or they passed responsibility on to someone else who did not, or who reversed their judgement. In effect, individuals, pairs and groups of individuals turned a blind eye to what was happening. They saw and did not see. They knew what they had to do, yet they failed to act. One professional decided one thing, while their colleague decided another. There was no communication about differences of opinion.

The main reason people behave like this is because they are conflicted about what they see or know. They have seen, or they know, but with one part of their mind they cannot accept that something so malign could be real. This is true of us all, not only of child welfare professionals. We are all likely to deny that we have seen something that we find too horrific to face. But people working in child protection are constantly required to deal with the reality that a child may be abused in ways that they cannot bear to contemplate. There is something literally 'unthinkable' happening when children are being seriously abused; yet we expect people who are faced with evidence of abuse to carry on thinking about the unthinkable, and to do so *without fail*.

Towards a modern relationship-based practice

In this pamphlet we argue that conflict or potential conflict is always at the heart of working with children at risk, and that people need help to work in situations of conflict.

Sometimes the conflict is in the mind of the practitioner; sometimes it is between the professional and the parents or carers. At other times it is between professionals, or between professionals and the courts. At the root of it there is the conflict between the adults and the child suffering maltreatment, though this may not appear on the surface as conflict because the child is often dependent and frightened.

The main thing that makes public services for children so challenging to organise and deliver is that they must centre on relationships, and these relationships involve people facing very painful and unwelcome realities. This may sound pessimistic, but a teacher, play worker, community nurse or GP never knows when she or he is about to be faced with the knowledge that child abuse may be happening. From the child's point of view, the capacity in the professionals to face this knowledge is as crucial in ordinary community settings, as it is for the specialist child protection social worker, paediatrician or police officer.

People need help with understanding and working through situations such as these, and they go on needing help no matter how experienced they are. The Victoria Climbié case showed this all too clearly. Later in this pamphlet we propose that negotiation and authority are central principles that should inform work with children at risk, at all levels. In part, this means that people need to feel sufficiently confident to assume the necessary authority to take the first step of naming the possibility of abuse, and following through with the consequences. The consequences usually involve conflict, but often without the support of a court order or even a child protection conference decision.

Negotiation, in circumstances of conflict, becomes essential. Taking appropriate authority, and staying in negotiation rather than backing off or taking premature controlling measures, requires skill, knowledge, courage, integrity and good professional judgement. This is what we mean by relationship-based practice. It concerns the necessity, and difficulty, of maintaining a balanced but purposeful stance in extremely testing conditions in ordinary frontline settings in the public sphere. Without attention to how we can construct a framework in public services for children that sustains and validates the importance of relationships, we do not believe that this work can be made safer or more effective.

The idea of relationship-based work was once primarily associated with therapeutic interventions in public sector contexts. We think that therapeutic skills and sensibilities are vital in work with children at risk of harm, their families and communities. But modern practice in the public sector means they must be deployed in new ways, and adapted to be useful in ordinary encounters in hospitals, schools, housing offices, playgroups and so on. In this pamphlet we do not discuss the nature of these skills in any depth. What we do discuss are the principles that could create the conditions in which they might develop and flourish.

The effect of tight resources

Resources are a contentious issue which breed poor morale among social workers and child protection staff. For many years, social workers were admonished that throwing money at problems did not solve them. Statistics suggest that child welfare absorbs ever increasing resources, while the practical experience of social workers is that there are never enough resources to be able to provide the nursery places, family centres, family aides and respite foster care that are needed. Assessments of children's needs are frustrated by a lack of resources to meet those needs. Above all there is not enough professional time. In comparison with other European countries, England spends less on prevention and allows social workers less time in which to do their work.

New sources of support for families are now being developed and some of the New Labour initiatives such as *Quality Protects, Sure Start* and the Children's Fund are beginning to make an impact. There are some problems of adjustment for social workers in that these resources are not so easy for them to access or control. There are also variations between districts: if you live in a relatively well to do area which is not eligible for some sources of funding, you may find it harder to access particular types of support.

However, it has been obvious for years that in England a great deal of money is spent on the process of bringing a case to court, which, if it had been available for supportive services, could have been used to prevent the need for court proceedings in the first place.

Lack of resources, or their allocation, has a very direct effect on the morale of child welfare professionals, and affects the way that they approach their task. Social work practitioners taking part in a comparative study discussed the impact on their thinking.[6] 'Resources – or lack of resources – begin to limit the whole way you think about something, the ideas that you can have. . . . Here you really have to argue for more funding based on risk, and there's a tendency to see risk more because it gives you more funding.'

The importance of cultural change

The ultimate aim needs to be to change the practice, cultures and behaviour of front line practitioners. Structural change aims to do this but often fails because the cultural forces holding the system together can withstand structural changes. Only when structural change coheres with cultural change will it impact on the functioning of the system.

Sometimes massive structural change can lead to very little change in functioning, but sometimes relatively small changes can have large-scale ramifications, especially if they open the floodgates to a change which needs to happen. Managers and policy-makers are drawn to structural change because that is what they are in charge of, and it can be done relatively quickly and easily. Cultural change is a much more risky, subtle process beset with unintended outcomes.

Cultural and systemic change in our child protection system will have to accommodate the realities of past practice and current expectations to a considerable degree. But systems and their cultures can accommodate change despite possible tensions with the surrounding context. In fact, no legal, organisational or policy culture is ever fully internally consistent. There are always spaces for change. Mostly it is a matter of political will, professional courage and a willingness to embrace creativity.

Rather than focusing on new techniques, structures or processes which will enable professionals to be more child-focused, or on new regulations to improve quality, we believe that efforts should be focused on three related principles which will not only improve practice but will result in children being better protected and professionals having more satisfactory working lives. The three principles are trust, authority and negotiation.

3. Trust, authority and negotiation: principles for a reformed system

We propose a new system of child welfare based on three organising principles: trust, authority and negotiation. It is important to note that these are not moral principles but 'systemic' principles, which describe how social systems can operate more effectively in dealing with the conflict involved in child welfare. Although we believe strongly that the system should be child-focused, sensitive to race and culture and embody fairness, these moral principles beg the question 'What sort of system can be more child focused?'.

It is also important for the system that the individuals within the system feel competent and able to make the system work. Thus more resources for the child protection system and for better training for workers are also very important. These are necessary but they are not all that is needed to produce a system that is safe for children and professionals. In order to achieve this, the system must address the three fundamental principles trust, authority and negotiation.

Three value positions lie behind our thinking on trust, authority and negotiation. Firstly, the welfare of the child may require not only that we listen to what the child says, but that we pay more attention to what she says, and allow the child's voice more weight. Secondly, the state, and the social worker as employee of the state, have a right to be concerned about the welfare of children within the family and therefore a right to make demands on parents. Thirdly, the state has a reciprocal duty to provide help for parents in meeting these demands.

If the state is going to demand more of parents, parents have a right to expect more from the state. The community in which parents function also has a right to expect that the state both supports parents and makes demands on them.

These value positions have important implications: the state, in pursuing its right to be concerned about the welfare of children, may need to take more action rather than less in relation to the demands that it makes on parents. At the same time, if attention is paid to the views of children, and if the state fulfils its duty to provide help to parents, this action may be low key, less intrusive and more supportive.

It must be emphasised that the views that we put forward are not intended to result in either more state intervention or less, but different. They are intended to increase the ability of services to respond to families in difficulties before protection becomes necessary.

This 'prevention of the need for protection' is the goal of government policy, as established in the DoH's *Framework for the Assessment of Children in Need and their Families.*[7] We support this aim, but emphasise that it will require an increase in resources and a reallocation of resources to be realisable. It is important for the system that the individuals within the system feel competent and able to make the system work. Thus, calls for more resources for the child protection system and for better training for workers are important, but they are not all that is needed to produce a system that is safe for children and professionals.

This also requires a cultural change, without which any new or existing resources will continue to be channelled into risk-driven responses. It is this cultural change that is the focus of our proposals.

What is required is a conceptual shift from a 'child protection' system to a 'child welfare' system: a system which responds to the needs of children for parenting that is good enough to enable them to grow up at the very least unharmed by their social, economic and emotional circumstances.

Trust

Trust can only be developed over time, even if it can be built on generalised trust in a service or institution. There is currently a lack of trust in relation to child protection services, and it is shaky in relation to child health and welfare systems more generally.

Trust (or lack of trust) is an element of the relationships between professionals and other professionals as well as between service users and professionals. Just as families need time to learn to trust workers, workers need time to learn to trust each other. We need a new basis on which to re-establish relationships of trust.

There are two components to trust, firstly, the belief that the other party has your own interests at heart, even if there is some conflict in the relationship, and secondly, the belief that what the other person says is true, that the person is acting in good faith.

With regard to welfare provision, trust at its most fundamental level involves a belief by the population that the state is basically benign, and that state services are essentially there for their benefit. This is notwithstanding the conflicts of interest which will inevitably emerge in welfare delivery. The state in turn must trust the families to bring up their children, and must be driven by the basic belief that families who need help are entitled to support by right, rather than that these families are failures in need of surveillance and monitoring. The state and the community should also feel able to trust professionals to exercise their professional judgement to assess and intervene when necessary and to ensure the fair and equitable distribution of resources.

There are many good reasons why our trust in traditional forms of trust has been shaken. The attack mounted on professional and trade union interest groups by the Conservative administrations of 1979 onwards coincided with the revelation that many of the neutral organs of the state actually serve the interests of vested elites. It was revealed that there are abuses of power inside the institutions in which we had placed trust.

The combined effect was devastating, rocking the foundations of the culture of welfare we knew. Professionals were no longer trusted by government, no longer felt trusted, and so lost faith in themselves and trust in one another. At the same time those in need of professional help still want to trust professionals, but they have been empowered to question professionals' expertise and judgement, eroding the previous trust they had.

Trust is the inalienable basis upon which helping relationships (even conflictual ones) are founded. We have to rediscover a revised basis for trust in seeking a new set of principles for child protection work. We cannot go back to old assumptions about the essential decency of the dedicated professional, trained within a vocational tradition. But neither can we move forward on the basis of a culture of institutionalised suspicion and surveillance.

Developing relationships of trust takes time. Social workers and other professionals need time to talk to children, to parents, and to each other. All parties have to have the chance to get to know each other before they can decide whether and in what respect they can trust each other. Families cannot decide how far they can trust the social services if they see a different worker every time. Professionals similarly need the opportunity to test out how far they can have confidence in each other's work. Developing a relationship of trust makes heavy demands on social work and other professional time but it has the potential to save time as well: time spent in conferences, in court hearings and in unsuccessful planning. Time spent on building trust, whether between workers and families or between agencies may have very little quantifiable value, but it is necessary for effective work with families and cooperation between professionals.

The need for conditional confidentiality

A principle of conditional confidentiality needs to govern processes in child protection. Trust cannot become established under conditions of initial suspicion and anxiety, without confidence that difficult and threatening disclosures will be treated confidentially. Sometimes, but actually only rarely, this will involve unacceptable risks so the conditions under which the principle of confidentiality is abandoned must be transparent. A principle of absolute confidentiality creates a trap for all involved, and tends to lead to its wholesale rejection. Confidentiality thus should be a negotiated matter.

The system as trustworthy

Public sector professionals should develop a culture that operates according to an impetus to act rather than a belief that intervention is inherently damaging and should occur only after meeting certain thresholds. This implies that child welfare services should be proactive and prepared, if right for their community, to operate outside the confines of the current social services structures and service locations.

Rigour, critique, confrontation, conflict, self-analysis and so on are all necessary subsidiary principles linking the behaviour and responsibility of individuals within systems, with the operation and development of the system itself. From the point of view of families, the system as well as the individuals needs to be trustworthy.

Mistakes and misjudgements should be primarily an occasion for learning from experience not for forensic or public enquiry. In this respect, the development of Part 8 reviews where the circumstances of child death or injury associated with abuse are independently reviewed as a basis for learning, is a step in the right direction.[8]

The total task of child protection needs to be understood as primarily an endeavour carried out by the system as a whole, not one of individual accountability or responsibility, although these are obviously present.

Organisations and institutions should be continually systematically self-examining, and helped to be so by independent processes and personnel functioning as critical friends. All professionals and working groups of staff are liable to become blinkered, defensive, inward-looking and internally conflicted. They need help to manoeuvre themselves out of such states, and understand the forces operating on them that encourage such retreat from the main task.

Non-intervention

The impetus not to intervene has been encouraged by the interpretation usually made of an important section in the Children Act 1989. The Act states that 'Where a court is considering whether or not to make one or more orders under this act with respect to a child, it shall not make an order or any of the orders unless it considers that doing so would be better for the child than making no order at all' (Children Act 1989 s 1 (5)). Of course the principle itself is valid. No one wants to see court orders being unnecessarily imposed. However, we disagree with the extension of this narrow principle into a general principle of non-intervention by the state.

In England, not intervening has been seen as better because it means not using compulsion; the idea that intervention can be voluntary and welcomed has faded. In some European countries positive steps are taken to promote preventive intervention and the boundary between the voluntary engagement and compulsion is clearly institutionalised.

Belgium and Germany both have clearly stated policies of promoting voluntary engagement that are supported by policy makers and professionals. In these countries a commitment to voluntary engagement does not imply non-intervention. It is based on the expectation that low level, local preventive services should be readily used.

The Child Abuse Centres of both the Flemish and Francophone Communities of Belgium (see page 68 – Work with a family at a Belgian Child Abuse Centre) and the Flemish Mediation Committee in Belgium (see page 71 – Negotiation and semi-compulsion) support voluntary engagement and provide space for reflection and negotiation before compulsory measures are instigated.

Germany has a service similar to the Child Abuse Centres, and a help-planning meeting to coordinate voluntary services. Both these countries have made the decision not to introduce mandatory reporting of child abuse.

These are the conditions in which trust in the welfare systems can be re-established, without that trust being blind. On the contrary, this form of trust entails a preparedness to make practice and functions transparent to examination, and in particular to self-examination.

It could be argued that developments such as the growth in audit, inspection and performance measurement of public services are precisely designed to improve public trust in institutions. Monitoring, the approach holds, is the attempt by government to improve services, thereby increasing the public's trust in them. This is based on the belief that the public is more likely to trust services if there are effective quality control mechanisms in place.

While there is certainly a need for public accountability of state services this approach has run its course. Increased regulation, monitoring, target-setting and inspection will do little now, either to improve the overall quality of services or to increase the public's trust in them. Quality assurance on its own provides only the illusion of quality and is based on the notion that welfare is a product just like hamburgers or toilet paper, and can be measured and its quality assured in the same way. Real quality in public services does not come from monitoring. To achieve it requires a change in the social contract.

Customer or client? A new trust relationship

There needs to be a re-examination of the current dominant metaphor of welfare: that welfare recipients are customers or consumers of a service. This notion has pervaded the public sphere and the delivery of personal social services for over a decade. It is based on choice and rights but not on trust. In fact customers in a commercial transaction are by definition at odds with the provider of the service. 'Quality assurance' to 'customers' in the private sector is mainly a way of ensuring more custom for the company. It is based on a negative view of rights, which are seen as rights to be free *from* unnecessary intervention, rather than rights *to* a service. It is not a mechanism for building trust with consumers. Trust involves mutual dependency and a willingness to forego some autonomy in return for being cared for.

But if we are to abandon the idea of children and families as customers, what are we to put in its place? One possible solution would be a return to the premanagerialist notion of 'client'. Until the 1980s the pervading metaphor was that practitioners were the experts and their clients trusted (or were forced to trust) their expertise. But it is not desirable or possible to go back to those days. As we have discussed, people will simply not trust experts in the way they have done previously. A different form of relationship needs to develop between professionals and users, and this needs to be based on a re-mandating of the professional role.

A key part of the process of revitalising the trust between child welfare professionals and the public is to provide opportunities for dialogue and negotiation between professionals and users. At one level this needs to happen between the professionals and the public. The professional role needs to be supplemented by a range of structures that move beyond quality control mechanisms, and create spaces or forums where families and professionals can engage in real dialogue.

This does not mean only involving users in the management boards of institutions such as the National Care Standards Commission or the Social Care Institute of Excellence. Nor does it mean only that users should be given satisfaction questionnaires or better complaints procedures. It calls for open meetings, consultation exercises or, more radically, the electing of lay members to Area Child Protection Committees.

Some of the more recent government initiatives such as *Sure Start*, the Children's Fund and *Connexions* require users and community members (including children and young people in the case of the latter two) to be part of local management partnerships. These initiatives are a move in the direction we are suggesting, although no such provisions were included in *Working Together to Safeguard Children* (1999) in relation to the Area Child Protection Committee or the child protection system more generally. We support this aspect of the initiatives proposed by the Local Government Association in their recent publication *Serving Children Well; a new vision for children's services.*[9]

Experiencing trust

All European child welfare services work with a legacy of distrust which carries over from the not so distant past, when children could be removed from their families, without their parents having much power to contest this, and often stayed in state care for the rest of their childhood. Parents still fear the power of the state to remove their children, and trust in child welfare institutions has to be built under adverse circumstances.[10]

A parent in Germany was very frightened of contacting the Jugendamt (child welfare department). She went to a local community agency, and with the support of the community worker, who acted as her advocate, she then managed to approach the department, who were able to offer help and spend time working with her on planning for her children's needs. Describing her experiences she commented that they had listened to her and that she had learnt to trust them. The response of workers had enabled her to overcome her considerable fear and distrust of the agency. She had used her positive experience to build a relationship that enabled her to co-operate actively with the agency in spite of later problems.

Thus, trust in an institution can be built and maintained in spite of initial anxieties and disagreements.

Another mother had a very hard time when her new partner seriously abused one of her children. Initially she had a lot of disagreements with her social worker. In spite of this she greatly appreciated the support that she was given not only by her social worker and but by the team as a whole. 'There was always someone there for me. I couldn't have managed without them.' Their disagreements did not prevent her from trusting both the worker with whom she had most contact, and the institution.

Trust is not built by social workers (or other professionals) giving families what they want, or encouraging dependency. Trust can be built in situations even where there is conflict or disagreement. With a basis of trust, people can tackle unpleasant problems or work together in spite of disagreements. Establishing and working with trust is not a soft option, but families appreciate this kind of trust relationship when they experience it.

A young mother had had a difficult life and she was now struggling to be able to keep her child. She understood that the social workers were concerned about her child and about herself, even though they were taking her to court. She described the social worker who had helped her most by saying 'she made me feel I could do things'. Her comment illustrates the reciprocal nature of trust; she had trusted the social worker and the social worker's trust in her had helped her to be more able to cope.

Interagency communication: trust between professionals

One of the major problems of the child protection system, and the welfare system generally, is the erosion of trust between different professionals and agencies that are charged with the protection of children. This has led to lack of communication, which has in turn led to failures to protect children. There are many reasons for this including decreasing resources, increasing bureaucracy, professionals guarding their own hierarchical positions and repeated structural changes across major services.

In order to provide a reasonable service to children it is imperative that professionals work together more effectively. This is a problem which has been recognised for a long time, but until recently the solution was only seen to be more interagency training and increasing numbers of protocols about information exchange and joint working.

There are other changes that could greatly increase professionals' trust in each other. In the same way that trust between professionals and families is not increased by rules, written agreements, complaints procedures or feedback forms, interprofessional trust is not improved by protocols, guidance or procedures. Trust is built through two interrelated processes: positive experiences of each other leading to positive expectations for the future, and good communication.

There are two key processes that need to be developed to promote trust. Firstly, there needs to be informal forums where professionals can discuss issues and cases which concern them. Secondly, professionals need to develop a capacity to understand and work with the different languages they use. The aspiration to develop a single common language among professionals in child protection is misplaced, because different languages reflect important differences in skill, method of work, and focus of intervention. What does need to be developed is a common *understanding* about child abuse and protection, which can accommodate differences of professional perspective.

Although it may sound like common sense that professionals should be able to discuss cases informally and learn from each other, recent legal and professional developments have made this more rather than less difficult. In particular, the Human Rights Act and the Data Protection Act have been interpreted as restricting the exchange of information between agencies. As a result, professionals are now far more reluctant to discuss cases.

One way forward would be for discussions to be anonymised, but this would present enormous practical difficulties. Far better would be a new interpretation of the legislation which would allow such exchanges if they were manifestly in the best interests of a child, and if they did not, in themselves, result in loss of rights to a parent.

The second point, language, is less often recognised as an issue, but has come to light in some of our comparative research in Europe. In some European countries, notably Italy and France, there is a theoretical stance which is shared by mental health professionals as a whole. This shared professional language is not the preserve of any particular profession or agency, and it allows more successful communication about families across agencies. In this country there is a lack of shared language in this respect, not only between professions but also sometimes within them. While it is not possible, in the short term, to change this, it is important to recognise it.

There may seem to be a contradiction between advocating changes which on the one hand are designed to increase confidentiality and on the other hand to increase interagency communication. The real point is that higher levels of trust between professionals in different agencies reduce the tensions between reporting and confidentiality.

The primary aim of any system must be to protect children, and effective child protection must be undertaken on an interagency basis. In the next section we introduce the concept of a confidential space where children and their parents could work on their problems without the immediate threat of child protection procedures.

The aim of confidential spaces is not to undermine these principles, but to improve their operation and to take a pragmatic and realistic approach. Ultimately the confidential spaces offered to children and families are there to allow them time to negotiate the terms on which the multiagency system will protect the child (or alternatively to resolve the issue and protect the child without involving other agencies). If professionals trust each other enough, and if there are sufficient checks and balances in the system, then the process will be perceived as safe by all the stakeholders.

Manadatory reporting and trust

In the past, communication issues around child abuse have been addressed in different countries in the world by the development of so called mandatory reporting laws or protocols. These laws operate in the USA, Canada, Australia and in many continental

European countries, although they differ considerably in each system. The common thread is that professionals such as doctors, teachers, social workers and youth workers are required by law to refer cases of suspected abuse to the child welfare services or police. They are likely to be disciplined or even charged if they fail to report.

Mandatory reporting can mean different things depending on the rules that govern what is reported and the attitude to intervention on the part of the professionals and the community. In the Nordic countries, where social workers and other professionals have to report suspicion of abuse as well as actual abuse, reporting is seen as an encouragement to introduce voluntary supportive and preventive interventions at an early stage. The community, on the whole, accepts it in this spirit.

Research on mandatory reporting has found that the actual laws around reporting seem to have less effect on professionals' willingness to report cases than the organisational culture of the professionals. It has been found, for example, that it is the training and publicity surrounding the introduction of mandatory reporting laws that has had the impact, rather than the law itself.[11] Higher levels of confidentiality often coexist with strict reporting laws. In some countries this has caused tension and difficulty. The Netherlands, for example, has had to reorganise its child protection system because of these problems. On the other hand there are many countries where these tensions are managed well, and the system operates satisfactorily for all.

Ultimately, mandatory reporting laws (and similar strict protocols in *Working Together to Safeguard Children*) can be seen in two opposing ways. They can be seen as a useful bolster for professionals who can feel confident that their efforts to protect children are undertaken within a supportive framework. They can also be seen as prescriptions from the government which impose on them an obligation to behave in a checklist way towards children and families, and which undermine their individual professional judgement. The difference is the overall level of trust between professionals.

Multidisciplinary working

Another way of increasing trust between professionals is for them to work together in multiagency or multidisciplinary teams. Working together on a day-to-day basis facilitates trust between professionals and creates understanding between them. While developing multidisciplinary teams or locating professionals in community contexts can be problematic, there are considerable benefits, not only for the professionals involved, but also for children and families.[12] Professionals become much more accessible, families can see a range of people in the same place, and services can be located in contexts which are less stigmatising for families.

In the 1970s it was fairly common for social workers to be based in health centres, schools, hospitals and other community locations. Over the past two decades, however, the trend has been for social workers to be pulled back into large teams based in town halls where they have increasingly provided a fire-fighting service, responding only to emergencies. This process was driven mainly by resource considerations, but it has resulted in a loss of trust between professional groups and also between professionals and communities.

The establishment of Youth Offending Teams, Behaviour and Education Support Teams and the further development of Child and Adolescent Mental Health services are a sign that policy is already moving back towards a more holistic and interdisciplinary approach, and the establishment of multiagency children's partnerships at strategic levels in many areas shows the potential for agencies to collaborate on planning and development of services as well as on delivery. Despite these welcome developments, mainstream children's services still tend to work largely in their own agency silos and interdisciplinary working is still the exception rather than the rule.

Trust within the community

One of the reasons why the child protection system is perceived by many potential users as being threatening and unfair is that it is perceived as operating to a professional agenda with little concern for the realities of people's real lives. Much of this is misconception, and the real situation is far more complex.

The findings of the Maltreatment Report are interesting in that there is a large discrepancy between the way that researchers defined abuse and the way victims of abuse defined that abuse.[13] This discrepancy is partly explained by abused children believing that the care they were receiving was normal, but is also due to the discrepancy between professional definitions and people's own experiences. Indeed, those few abused children who did receive help from professionals were overwhelmingly critical of it.

There have been some notable recent developments in government's attempts to involve community members in the development of policy and practice, and some of these show real promise. Many of the more recent government initiatives such as *Best Value*, *Sure Start*, the Children's Fund, *Quality Protects* and *Connexions* have made the involvement of parents and young people themselves important parts of their programmes.

There are three basic reasons for this resurgence in user participation, all of them very relevant to the development of effective child protection systems, and all are attempts to increase trust in government. Firstly, user participation gives an initiative validity with its intended recipients, many of whom are suspicious of government and its attempts at social engineering. Secondly, it represents an attempt by central government to respond directly to the people on whom it is spending money without the mediation of local government, which can be regarded as rather obstructive. Thirdly, it is a communitarian response to what government sees as the breakdown of civil society and an attempt to involve citizens in the democratic process in new ways.

But user involvement has turned out to be more difficult than was imagined, with many attempts regarded as tokenistic or ill thought out. Nevertheless, government has recognised that the involvement of users and community members is an essential component of the future of governance and service provision in the 21st century.

In a new child protection system the lessons learned in the past few years of user involvement are crucial. In particular, parents and children must be involved in designing the way the child protection system operates in their local areas as well as being involved as community representatives in decision-making about the system. Some suggestions for this may include:

- consultation with service users and others about definitions of abuse and the appropriate responses which should be taken in different sorts of scenarios
- community members being part of the confidential and negotiative structures
- community members being involved in case conferences
- community members sitting on Area Child Protection Committees.

This sounds radical, but Scotland has for many years had lay members on its Children's Panel, and this has been successful. Of course there are many issues to be worked out, such as confidentiality issues arising from having neighbours involved in decisions about one's life, but these are practical problems which have been overcome in other countries, and are not insuperable.

Community involvement should not be seen as a risk-free strategy. Several authors have advocated the community development approach as a panacea to our current problems, seeing empowerment of women and children as the way of resolving the conflicts and difficulties in the system.[14] That is not our analysis. Conflict and contradiction are inherent in child protection, and we see community involvement as one way of positively addressing the conflict. But in itself, community involvement is not the solution. Although safeguarding children is a community issue, the child protection system must ultimately be run by professionals who have as much legitimacy, and with it authority, from the community as possible.

Authority

Social workers and other child welfare professionals inevitably embody the authority of the state when they intervene to provide services set up by the state to compel actions for the well-being of the child. This authority needs to be recognised and accepted as part of the role of the professional, who is representing the state's view of the best interests of its future citizens. Authority can be accepted and indeed welcomed if it is used openly and sensitively and within a context of some level of trust. Where there is no trust, authority can only be imposed, and it becomes coercion.

Authority can derive from many sources. Coercive authority derives from the power of the law, which allows professionals to take families to court and recommend children being removed. Authority also derives from the professional role itself: the expertise and knowledge of the professionals gives them authority, as does their access to other professionals and services. Personal authority is also fundamental to the professional relationship, and derives from the day-to-day encounters with children and families. These sources of authority can be in tension with or can reinforce each other.

Social workers and authority in France

French social workers are very impressed by the power of English social workers. English parents too feel that social workers are very powerful. But English social workers feel powerless, and lack confidence in their effectiveness and authority.

In the French child welfare system, authority and power is very clearly located with the Judge for Children, who deals with both child welfare and youth offending cases. The social workers that work for the Children's Judge are not local authority employees. In some ways these workers do not have as much power as English social workers, but they do not feel powerless (as English social workers do), because they represent the delegated power of the Judge, and this is recognised by the families they work with. They do not formally have power, but they have authority.

> Children are usually referred to the court by the local authority social services department. However, professionals in other services (doctors, nurses, teachers) can also make a referral, and family members, including children can refer themselves. In the context of an inquisitorial legal system, the judge represents the victim, so the Children's Judge represents the child and has wide terms of reference:'If the health, safety, or morality of a minor are in danger or if the conditions of his or her upbringing are seriously compromised, the judiciary may make orders for help with the child's upbringing' (Civil Code). The hearings are informal and take place in the Judge's office. Lawyers are rarely involved and no other officials like court clerks or ushers are present. The audience is likely to last from half-an-hour to an hour.
>
> The Children's Judge can make a range of orders, including placement in care, but the supervision order is the most common. The supervision order (*Action Educatif au Milieu Ouvert* – AEMO) is a contract between the family and the state for the work to be done and the services to be provided. A large number of AEMO orders are renewed or extended at the request of the parents.
>
> The combination of an informal (and relatively unthreatening) system and wide terms of reference leads to a high level of referral into the judicial system, so that a lot of work is done with families under the umbrella of the Judge's power. In situations where the law is not involved, the French social worker has the authority that derives from a general recognition of the validity and professionalism of the social work role.[15]

The ability of practitioners to use authority effectively derives from their position as agents of the state and it depends on trust. Firstly, trust between the policy-makers and professionals: professionals need to have confidence in the congruence between their view and that of the policy-makers. Secondly, trust between practitioners and the parents and children who they work with: if a basis of trust is lacking, authority lacks a basis for negotiation, and compulsion is likely to be the only way forward.

Thus, trust and authority are closely connected. The trust has to be earned (both by the worker and the parent), while the authority of the worker derives from an agreed and shared perception of the role of the state in relation to children. Authority, and confidence in authority, is a basic requisite for working in situations of risk. Authority is also closely linked to accountability: unaccountable authority is authoritarian and elitist.

Support and suspicion

At the core of the problem of child welfare systems is the need for practitioners, and therefore the system, to be open to working in both a supportive and suspicious frame of mind at the same time. This is in addition to the need for practitioners to hold in mind the complexity of the case they are dealing with, and the different and competing needs of family members.

Professionals need to understand and to be able to manage the boundary between being authoritative and the arbitrary exercise of power. In order to do so professionals must be self-aware, flexible and sensitive to the factors underlying their own and the family's behaviour and emotions. Supervision is crucial.

The tensions between suspicion and support address, but go way beyond, the care versus control tensions that are integral to all welfare provision. While there is a continuum from care to control, there is not a continuum from support to suspicion. Supportive relationships are based on trust; suspicious relationships are based on mistrust. Trust can occur within the context of a suspicious relationship but it is conditional and tentative. Managing these tensions is central to the professional skill of the social worker.

The fundamental dilemma for practitioners, therefore, is that child protection is not just carried out on a continuum from care to control but requires them to manage two incompatible ways of thinking about the work.

On one level child protection is just one component of welfare provision while at another level it is subject to different guidance and different laws, and most fundamentally, a completely different mind frame. From one perspective protection can be seen as one of many needs which children can have. The abuse a child is suffering may be less important to the child than her other problems such as bullying, housing, bereavement or immigration. On this level, child protection work can be integrated into child welfare and into a more holistic approach to family work. On another level, child protection is completely different and involves risk assessment, surveillance and suspicion.

Research shows that it is very difficult for practitioners and systems to move between these mind frames. Once a decision has been made that this is a case of family support, information tends to be filtered by this assumption. Similarly, if child abuse is suspected, information is tested against this basic assumption.

Negotiation

Most child welfare and child protection work takes place at a time when there are potentially many different ways for a situation to develop, and many alternative ways of promoting change. Before compulsion needs to be used, there is room for negotiation. We see negotiation as the default mode, the frame of mind in which all interactions should be approached unless compulsion is clearly necessary.

The process of protecting children involves power, and while the state appears to hold the power, the social workers who act for the state often feel powerless. Parents and children who refuse to co-operate can hold a negative power to prevent interventions from taking place. Ultimately the state has more power than the parent, the child has less power than anyone. But paradoxically the child has more power, as the centre of concern and potentially the source of knowledge about what has happened or is happening.

In child protection power is not evenly disbursed, and the position is complicated by the split in our system between child protection and family support. To designate a case as family support means to locate power with the parents. To designate a case child protection shifts power (except for some negative power) from the parents to the state. This shift is often abrupt, and from the point of view of the family members bewildering; for them, nothing may have changed. Their loss of power may be unexpected and unheralded.

The aim of negotiation is to provide an alternative space where the oncoming conflict can be foreseen, named, discussed and possibly averted. It is to do more than bridge the gap between family support and child protection. It is to foster the development of a continuum that is called child welfare. Negotiation in child welfare is based on trust and authority. Unless there is some level of trust, negotiation is pointless, because the agreements reached will not stick. Authority is present because the power between the parties is not equal, but negotiation implies some readiness on the part of one party to be influenced by the arguments of the other party, and thus to cede some power.

The place of negotiation in the Flemish child protection system[16]

Negotiation is not the same as either arbitration or mediation. Arbitration implies that the parties to the dispute have agreed to accept (or will be forced to accept) the outcome decided by the arbitrator, but that there is not necessarily a right decision. Mediation implies that the parties are equal and that any outcome will be the result of the debate between the parties, enabled but not influenced by the mediator. True mediation is not possible when one party, the child, is powerless and is not fully able to take part. Nevertheless, negotiation uses many of the same skills as mediation.

The most fully institutionalised use of negotiation in Europe is in the Flemish child welfare system. In setting up a new child welfare system in the 1980s, the Flemish community of Belgium arrived at a unique structure called the Mediation Committee, which must intervene before a case is referred to court.

In Belgium, most child welfare services are provided by charities and other non-governmental organisations. The services and the social service for children and families only work with families on a voluntary basis. If there is disagreement with parents about what should happen and the workers consider that there is need for compulsion, the family must be referred to the Mediation Committee. The social services cannot (except in an emergency) refer a family direct to the court.

Each Mediation Committee is made up of three lay mediators with some relevant professional knowledge or expertise, who see all families who are referred to the courts, except where there is an emergency. Referrals come from the Special Youth Assistance Service or from family members. The grounds for referral are wide; it is only necessary that there is 'a problematic educational situation: a condition, in which the physical integrity, the affective, moral, intellectual or social developmental chances of the minors (i.e. the under-aged) are negatively affected due to special event, relational conflicts or the circumstances, in which they live'.

The role of the Mediation Committee is to attempt to agree a solution to the problem and to mediate between parents, their children and the social workers. If this is not possible, or if a previously brokered solution breaks down, the Mediation Committee can decide that no further action is required. If they think that there is a need for intervention, and agreement cannot be reached, they must refer the case to the courts. A court order can only take place when no agreement has been reached through voluntary intervention and the child is in danger.[17]

One of the problems with the Flemish system is that it is hard to find suitable and suitably qualified lay Mediation Committee members to take on the task (it shares this problem with the Scottish Children's Panels). For this and other reasons, the Flemish government is in the process of exploring and piloting possible changes to the system.

Negotiation enables risks to be fully and openly assessed. It is a less intimidating process than investigation and prosecution, and thus less likely to generate a defensive and secretive response, and is less likely to generate the defensive closure of the family group and of the professional group. Negotiation encourages a less defensive and more open response from both the family and the professionals.

Negotiation requires a degree of trust between the parties to the negotiation and can also lead to improved trust as partners get to know and respect each other. True negotiation also implies that all the parties have some space for manoeuvre – there has to be a process of give and take on both sides rather than one side manipulating or exercising power over the other. It requires flexibility, a willingness to listen to the other's point of view. But perhaps the most important attribute of negotiation is that it requires the confidence to work with uncertainty and risk. When a solution to a problem is negotiated it very rarely provides a guarantee to any party, and the parties all have to accept that the solution is less than optimal from their point of view. They may have to compromise short-term security with the hope that the long-term solution to the problem will be more secure than it would have been if power had simply been exerted, for example to protect a child.

Negotiation and its difficulties

Negotiation also has its risks. One is that too much flexibility can lead to lack of judgement, drift and collusion. Another is that where negotiation takes place between the powerful parties to the case, the less powerful parties (almost invariably the children) are not real participants. It can also lead to the easy way out where everybody gets something but actually the problem is not resolved. This can be extremely dangerous, and this kind of adult-focused negotiation is often found in the most serious cases of abuse, when parents, either consciously or unconsciously, lead the workers to believe that they are cooperating but where they are in reality subverting the negotiation and continuing to abuse the child. Equally, workers may be tempted into buying off the felt risks of serious and prolonged confrontation through a weak negotiated solution.

A further risk is that the negotiation becomes circular and eventually becomes stalemated. This is not serious when the parties realise that this is happening and they can then break out of the immediate confrontation and go for mediation to a more objective or authoritative person (or institution). Much more dangerous is when parties believe they are negotiating but actually they are merely re-stating previous positions in a different way. This kind of situation is well known in family work, for example when alcoholic or violent spouses continuously promise that this will be the last time, but at another level everybody knows that the pattern will continue.

This means that negotiation must not become an end in itself. It should be purposeful and it should be conducted within well-defined parameters. For negotiation to be successful, it is important that checks and balances are put in place to ensure there is real participation by all parties.

Negotiation also needs to be undertaken between different professional groups. Most child protection commentators identify communication rather than negotiation as the key to safe child protection practice. It is obvious that effective child protection requires good communication between professionals, but we believe that trust and negotiation must underpin that communication. Many inquiries into serious abuse have identified the lack of status of some front line workers as one of the important factors that led to important information being discounted. An effective child welfare system would have to involve lower-status professionals being seen as credible partners in the process of information sharing about families, and being able to negotiate with other professionals.

Supervision – holding the tension

Working with children at risk involves holding a number of principles in continuing complex tension. This is psychologically and organisationally demanding, and there are always significant pressures to either act too soon, or not soon enough. Different members of the total system (the child, the carers, the extended family, the network of professionals) will hold different perspectives on what ought to be done, and different aspects of the anxiety about any course of action. The capacity to go on thinking, without turning a blind eye, and without a precipitate rush to action needs to be supported if it is to remain consistent and intelligent in the face of these pressures.

The best means of ensuring that the individual practitioner is not drawn into the system of the abusing family, and is able to maintain a balance between suspicion and support, is the provision of critical and supportive supervision. Good practice is hardly possible if workers do not have some space where they can stand back from the immediate task and think through their actions and the implications of their actions, and no one can reliably and consistently do this without help. There are many different ways that such supervision can be provided, but whatever the means by which this is done, it is the most reliable way of enabling front line practitioners to manage the tensions created by the conflicting needs of the families they work with and act with. It also allows them to act with confidence and professional authority.

The term supervision is a difficult one because it is defined differently in various professions. It is generally used in the social welfare professions to describe an opportunity for a worker to discuss the progress or lack of progress of his work (with individuals or groups) with a person who is able to help him to stand back from the pressures of the current situation and think about alternative approaches and about the possibly unacknowledged impact of his own anxieties and previous experience on his actions. It is important that supervision should be confidential, as the worker needs to be able to acknowledge (and learn from) his mistakes. A worker's line manager may be able to offer something of this. But a line manager has other pressures in relation to the same cases, and it is usually hard for her to be sufficiently disengaged from her management responsibilities to offer the right conditions for acknowledging mistakes, fears and anxieties. Ideally the supervisor should be an experienced worker who is not the line manager. Issues of confidentiality are important and the agency needs to have a clear policy about this. There are alternative ways of providing some opportunity for analysis and reflection. Both group supervision and peer supervision are useful here. The central task of the professionals is to create and sustain maximum openness for as long as this is still consistent with the best interests of the child. But they can do this only if they are capable of remaining open themselves.

To summarise, the factors that have to be held in complex interplay are:

- the tendency of abusive or risk-laden systems involving children to close down on themselves
- the interactional and reflective work required to sustain their openness, and the openness of the professional system
- the need to work and respond differentially over time, because the state of systems changes and evolves
- the need to keep the interests, experiences and circumstances of children in the foreground of thinking and decision-making, but not to separate these from attention to system factors
- the need to accept, and work clearly with conflicts in the child's system, not see them as an obstacle or intrusion in what ought to be a consensus
- the need to maximise capacity to take risks without endangering children, which entails the capacity of the system continually to tolerate and think about anxiety, conflict and uncertainty.

This is how many child protection teams, specialised assessment services, family centres and therapeutic resources already try to work. But many do not, or find they cannot. And most of the important local and national institutions in child protection are not designed to enable these principles to be readily implemented. The reasons for this relate to the history of child protection policy, but these problems are also a function of wider issues about how we generally conceive public services and welfare provision in Britain.

4. Risk and accountability: new principles for a new era

An underlying premise of this pamphlet is that the social contract between the state, professionals, and citizens stands in need of radical reinvigoration. At present, government's anxieties about performance are dominating the contractual agenda, while they are masked with rhetoric about user participation and empowerment. The fact is that users and professionals are in constant, complex and frequently turbulent contact every hour, of every day, of the working week. It is here, at this interface, that the social contract is actually enacted, produced and reproduced. And it is here, in our view, that matters are failing radically, while vast resources aimed at monitoring and auditing the quality of service delivery are spun to tell a different story.

A commitment to genuinely reinvigorating the nature of relationships, so that users are empowered through negotiation and authorised to take risks with their own lives, itself involves risk. But this is the challenge we believe must be met: to counter the risk society with a capacity to take risks, rather than be imprisoned by them.

Introducing change that involves reducing regulation is anxious work. Fears for the physical safety of children seem to increase as the reality of the dangers to their safety decrease, and these fears (which the authors share) make it hard for any public servant to suggest the reduction of procedures which were set in place with the express intention of reducing risk. Fear of failure has been the major shaping force of child protection practice in England and Wales for several decades. A non-accidental child death is a classic instance of a low probability/high consequence risk of the kind that is now understood to create risk averse cultures and practices in all walks of life. As one commentator puts it 'Risk society has an inherent tendency to become a scapegoat society'.[18]

Our argument is that trust between those creating and those preventing risk is the best and surest foundation for achieving risk reduction, and that negotiation between these parties in risk-laden circumstances affecting children is more likely to lead to sound judgements about risk, than the application of risk-assessment schemata drawn from non-comparable areas of professional life.

The weakness of risk aversion

All failures in child protection could be deemed failures of risk management or risk assessment, whether these concern instances of insufficient protection or excessive intervention to effect protection.

But success in this field is not symmetrical with failure: the risks taken in *not* intervening when intervention was nevertheless possible, and which prove retrospectively justifiable, go largely unremarked. A risk-averse culture of practice will always tend towards more extreme intervention later rather than less extreme intervention sooner. This creates secondary risks which also go largely unremarked.

Systems of risk assessment and management are oriented almost entirely to minimising risk of extreme failure, and never to promoting creative and acceptable risk taking in pursuit of good outcomes for children. Equally, the systems of professional accountability which have developed in tandem with the risk-averse culture, are almost exclusively oriented to locating responsibility and blame and accounting for error and failure, and almost never to encouraging responsibility (in the sense of autonomy) or acknowledging the inevitability of failure. In short, these methodologies are ill adapted to the complexity, uncertainty and indeterminacy of the functions to which they are applied.

This state of affairs stems from the misapplication of models of risk management and accountability from areas of professional life such as accountancy, car manufacture, or pollution control to areas of life in which risk has a completely different character.

Risk is not the same in something like child protection work, because human actors rather than smoke particles, gear boxes or expenditure flows are the sole object of concern. Risks have to be conceptualised completely differently; they are a function of interaction between those creating risks and those trying to prevent them, and not of control, management or elimination. Equally, they depend absolutely upon the exercise of judgement and interpretation in continually changing circumstances.

Welfare interventions contain both explicit and implicit risks. The most explicit risk is the weighing up of the risks of intervention (splitting up families, trauma for children) with the risks of non-intervention (continued abuse). Implicit risks include the risks to third parties (siblings, neighbours). Sometimes secondary risks like these are known, and can be weighed up at the time decisions are made, but others are much more subtle, and cannot be calculated. And there are risks for the practitioner, of which the main one is the possibility of getting it wrong either by intervening too coercively, or failing to intervene decisively enough. This is generally known as the 'damned if we do / damned if we don't' syndrome. Public enquiries are perhaps the best example of what professionals fear will happen to them if they get it wrong.

However, this well-known dilemma is not the only one for practitioners. Other perceived professional risks include stepping over professional or organisational boundaries. By intervening in cases where risk is low, professionals are potentially preventing other more serious cases from being dealt with and can be seen as misusing scarce resources. The irony of the situation, that by not intervening they allow more serious problems to develop which will cause more difficulty later, is one of which practitioners are well aware. But the agency imperative is much too powerful for them to do anything about it. This risk is increased when intervention requires some form of power or coercion, for example where the parent is hostile to intervention.

Thinking the unthinkable

One reason child abuse is so risky to professionals is its politicisation, and consequently the media attention which it attracts. Another is the intense emotion which child abuse engenders in us all, including child protection professionals. Child abuse, especially sexual abuse and child homicide, touches aspects of our personalities which we would rather leave alone. For most people, welfare professional and the public alike, it is relatively easy to imagine lashing out at a persistently demanding, whining or defiant child when under stress. Torturing a child, or deliberately targeting a child for sexual abuse, is in a different category altogether, both morally and emotionally. The intense emotions raised by such acts drive us into anger or denial. Professionals need to deal with these emotions, because if they are not acknowledged and dealt with, professional judgement can be severely affected.

So practitioners find it relatively easy to deal with the more obvious risks, even when these are high. Severe bruising, disclosure of sexual abuse or severe neglect are relatively straightforward for professionals to respond to because the expectation on them is clear. Where the risks are implicit rather than explicit, the factors more difficult to weigh up, or the case is complex and there is no clear 'binary' choice to be made about risk, professionals feel much less confident and tend to fall back into denial, optimism, a checklist mentality or the use of other unhelpful defensive risk avoidance techniques.[19]

However, comparative studies of child protection in other European countries have shown that it is possible to treat risk somewhat differently than we currently do in the UK. Here we take a case management approach to the work, which is characterised by risk assessment or risk avoidance, whereas other countries tend to take a therapeutic approach, in which risk is not a primary pre-occupation.

The case management approach tends to manage risk by diagnosis rather than responding to risk by building up relationships and therefore basing intervention on trust and authority. There is no absolute division between these two approaches. It is very likely that if one asked practitioners in England whether their aim was to build trusting relationships with their clients, the answer would be 'yes'. However, the English system makes this hard because it pushes practitioners away from personal relationship with users towards more formalised relationship based on procedures and rights.

Our rule of pessimism

Risk assessment is not only a formal process or activity. It is also a frame of mind and an approach to the work. It was striking that, in our comparative research, workers in English-speaking countries tended to focus on criteria for involvement such as eligibility and thresholds, the boundaries between agencies, and budgetary responsibility. When discussing the family itself they tended to focus on the short-term consequences of action or inaction, and whether action was justified. The preoccupation was therefore with thresholds and interventions.

In contrast to this, practitioners in many European countries first aimed to establish a good relationship between the workers and parents, the rationale being that only by doing so would they be able to help the family in the long term. They were concerned to work with and understand client's subjectivity, rather than to categorise and label behaviour or risk factors. They acknowledged the risks inherent in this approach, but risks did not disable or hinder their interventions. They were more able to work with uncertainty. Their approach could be seen to increase the danger, but from their point of view the risks of intervening too early in a statutory manner were even higher.

This therapeutic or relationship-based approach is based on very different premises to the English one. It sees the major task of child protection as gaining the trust of the family and the biggest risk to lose that trust. The context of work in those countries where a therapeutic approach is used is one that validates the authority of social workers in child welfare, both as representing the state and as professionals.

In England, professional optimism and confidence have been

undermined progressively over the past 20 years by a succession of political and media attacks. Practitioners and managers question the efficacy and equity of its traditional methods, especially the therapeutic approaches, which have been attacked from the right as lacking cost-effectiveness and an evidence base, and by the left as demonstrating bourgeois, patriarchal and ethnocentric attitudes towards service users. This has led to a generalised pessimism about the effectiveness of professional intervention and the ability of social workers and other professionals to effect change.

In response, English professionals have become much more pessimistic about the abilities of parents and to some extent now act according to a rule of pessimism which declares that parents are unlikely to change and that intervention is unlikely to succeed. Thus the case management approach combines pessimism about the benefits of intervention with pessimism that families can change. Professionals feel most comfortable intervening in a crisis when there is little choice for either party. In these circumstances there is very little risk because the intervention is a rescue. Rescue is a low-risk intervention because when a child or adult is rescued it seems axiomatic (although it is not) that the outcome of the intervention will be more positive than the risk of not intervening.

Another factor in the increasing pessimism of professionals is the resourcing of child protection work. There is not a linear relationship between risk and the availability of resources. Rather, risk is largely a matter of perception. However, resources have been diminishing for many years, and in the UK there has been a steadily increasing number of children and families in poverty and requiring welfare services. This has been combined with constant structural reorganisations designed to provide the same level of service for less money, while at the same time directing expenditure towards 'heavy end' concerns and away from preventive work. These factors come together to create inward-looking and organisation-obsessed health and social services structures. It is this perception of increasing need and decreasing resources which is particularly damaging for professional self-confidence and which raises the perception of risk.

Standards and quality in a complex world

By placing our faith primarily in principles rather than procedures, protocols, service standards and the whole armoury of modern instruments of public sector governance, we open ourselves to the charge of abandoning attention to standards and quality in the work. This is a genuine dilemma, but not one that can be successfully resolved by subjecting it to a simple either/or analysis.

Child welfare and child protection work is necessarily complex, uncertain and value-laden. It is complex not just because it is very complicated, with many factors in play at any one time, but also because it is always conducted within systems that are non-linear, dynamic and open-ended. It is the relationships between all the actors (including children) in this system that actually constitute the system. The system is not something independent of these people, although some of the principles shaping the behaviour and thinking of the actors will be independent of the actors.

For example, a protocol relating to the conduct of assessments will guide the behaviour of practitioners towards similar activities in different cases. But this protocol cannot determine the functioning of the total set of relationships and activities in play. If a parent decides to be difficult and obstructive of the assessment, the practitioner must deal with this and not expect the protocol to somehow magically solve the difficulty. The protocol, as an instrument guiding behaviour, is itself part of the system, not something that is applied to the system in the hope that it will work better.

Yet the whole structure of contemporary quality assurance and governance in the public sector is predicated on the assumption that the systems are broken, inefficient, badly maintained, and must be fixed with the aid of manuals and wiring diagrams that the mechanics must learn and obey.

This doesn't work for at least three reasons. Firstly, the introduction of the manual is an intervention within the system itself, not something that remains external to it. It becomes part of the continual and complex adaptive feedback process of the operation of the system itself.

Secondly, in child welfare work we are dealing with relatedness as the central unfolding process. The state of the system (whether at the micro or macro levels) is a function of the unfolding of relationships, and so is inherently unpredictable (but not thereby incapable of being purposefully influenced).

Thirdly, the manuals (guidance, procedure, inspection and inquiry reports, protocols) are static instruments that offer thin descriptions of thickly textured and dynamically evolving processes. Bluntly, they are not up to the job they are designed to do.

We suspect that the policy-makers' and politicians' nightmares are that if they accept this, then they will be ceding to chaos. The fantasy is that the only alternative to methodologies of control is no methodologies at all and hence no control. But this is not the case. If good child welfare and protection work is a function of good enough resources deployed within sensible structures, according to principles of the kind we have elaborated, then local systems will have patterns of functioning – of success, difficulty, occasional radical failure, innovation, stasis and so on. They will be the outcome of an interplay between local conditions and wider factors such as structure and resourcing.

The culture of a local system is generated in this way, and cannot be isolated from structure, relationship, community, local political/environmental, and macrosystemic factors. Viewed in this way, standards and quality must be evaluated and addressed as the product of the continual dynamic evolution of system complexity. Efforts to enhance standards will only work if they are themselves designed and implemented as true systemic interventions. Otherwise they act primarily to disturb and disrupt the whole system, its strengths as much as its weaknesses, thereby prejudicing the chances of improvement.

Quality assurance and governance methodologies need to adapt to respect and respond to this state of affairs, or they will be rapidly discredited.

New methodologies that take the system's complexity as their premise could be developed easily enough. They would involve those charged with inspection and standards working alongside the system, operating as a part of it, initiating and engaging in feedback processes, taking account of the many unpredicted and unpredictable influences that arise to influence the system, as well as those influences deriving from planned and rational intervention. The costs of methodologies like these need be no greater, and are probably lesser, than the burden of current quality assurance and governance costs. And they are likely to prove more effective, because they are adapted to the reality of the systems they are aiming to influence.

5. Lowering the ante: applying the three principles

In this section we move from the three fundamental principles on which a child welfare system should be based, to looking at the application of those principles in practice.

We propose two practical ways of developing the present child protection system according to these principles. One is to establish confidential spaces, in which families, children and professionals can explore their complex dilemmas within delimited and understood boundaries of confidentiality. The other is to establish negotiation forums, in which formal steps are taken towards resolving a conflict without recourse to more compulsion than is necessary.

The underlying rationale for these institutions is that they provide an opportunity for families to sort out their problems and conflicts by building trust with a skilled professional. In order to do so, the instruments of compulsory state intervention, the police and the law, are kept at bay for a limited and defined period so that issues can be resolved without 'upping the ante'. The purpose of both these institutions is to open up spaces which create more flexibility and opportunities for families to change.

Confidential spaces

The problems around confidentiality in the delivery of human services of all kinds have become acute, and may have reached a crisis point. This is because the issue is at the centre of two conflicting principles. On the one hand, confidentiality is deemed to be a fundamental part of the professional/client relationship and is essential if this relationship is to be built on trust. On the other hand, child welfare and child protection can only be undertaken if information is shared between professionals, and this cannot always be done with consent. In working with children this is complicated by the fact that both children and parents may have claims to confidentiality, and these may conflict.

While we do not propose a principle of absolute confidentiality, in the establishment of confidential spaces we are advocating a structure in which children who are concerned about their own safety can speak to a professional and try to resolve the issues without triggering a full blown investigation which they did not want or invite. Similarly, parents who have concerns about their own behaviour, or their feelings towards their children, should be able to discuss them in confidence without the fear that the child will be removed as a result.

There should be facilities where children and/or their parents can explore their complex dilemmas, and receive counselling and support for a limited time. Within the facility, the child would have ultimate say as to what action is taken to protect him/her for the limited time in which the facility is available. Questions about who should be involved in the response, and the course of action to be taken, would also be negotiated with the child. Parents would be offered a similar facility, and again would receive help for a limited period under specific conditions without the situation being referred further. It would be made clear that in an emergency, if the child's immediate safety were at risk, the professionals would act to protect the child.

It is important that these confidential spaces are managed within an overall professional structure and culture which values and promotes trust and information sharing between professionals. The existence of confidential spaces should not give rise to a general belief among professionals that it is acceptable to provide services to children at risk without informing the proper authorities. Indeed, there need to be specific guidelines on how the issue of confidentiality should be dealt with in the contexts of therapy, counselling, medicine and psychiatry.

The structure of a confidential space

In order for this structure to work, it would have to have the following features:

- It should be staffed by a multidisciplinary team of competent and trained professionals who are able to act authoritatively. Families are often very resistant to change, and professionals will have to engage with them and persuade them of the necessity for change. But this facility is not just a talking shop, nor a confessional. Professionals will have to be skilled in assessing whether real change has taken place, and will also need to know how to put in place programmes which will enable change to be maintained.
- Supervision should be provided for all professional staff. Supervision, on top of management, but distinct from it, is not an optional extra for the success of such a service. It is crucial.

Parents and children should be told exactly what the parameters of the service which they are being offered are, the duration and the rules. They need to know the limits of confidentiality and the consequences of non-cooperation. Inevitably, a number of people will try to use such a facility for their own ends, and it must be made clear that this will not be acceptable; they must cooperate with the professionals or eventually face a less negotiated form of intervention.

- Professionals themselves must be aware of the rules and must stick to the remit of the institution. The role of supervision and management is to ensure that they do not collude with families who continue to place children at risk.

The team should be multidisciplinary, with at least health and social services input. The confidential institution should have clear links with other parts of the child protection system, in particular the police, the social services departments and health authorities. These protocols would state how referrals should be made to the confidential service, how information should be shared between agencies when necessary and how cases will be passed from the confidential service to other agencies.

The exact structure and makeup of the service could be determined locally, but it should be required that each local authority have such an institution. However, the service should not be located at the offices of the social services department (or any agency with statutory child protection responsibilities). It should be on neutral ground, where families can make an approach without feeling stigmatised.

Work with a family at a Belgian Child Abuse Centre

Our ideas about the organisation and structure of a confidential space have been influenced by Belgian Child Abuse Centres, previously known as the Confidential Doctor Service.

The Belgian child welfare system has developed services that provide a therapeutic resource for families where there is abuse or anxiety about abuse. Parents or children can refer themselves, or may be persuaded to accept referral by another agency. Attendance is voluntary, and the service is not strictly confidential. The family members are told that if the child is in danger, action will be taken, if necessary through the courts. The work is undertaken by a multidisciplinary team who work closely together and provide peer support and supervision. The work with the family is intensive and can be long term. The work is firmly child-centred, and children have more say in the decisions to be made than they would in England.

A young woman, Natasha, contacted the child abuse centre because she was anxious about her younger sister. Natasha had left home, but lived in the same town as her family. She thought that their father was sexually abusing her younger sister, Sylvie (aged 13). Sylvie agreed to meet the social worker at Natasha's flat, on condition that her parents were not told. When she met the social worker, Sylvie said that she was being abused, but that she did not want her father to leave home. She then agreed that the social worker could talk to her parents. The social worker arranged to meet the parents. When they met, the father would not admit that anything was wrong, and said that it was just games. The social worker said that she disagreed with him; she said that she took it very seriously and that it was not just games. They agreed to further meetings.

After a number of meetings with different members of the family and with the parents there was a family meeting, which was observed by the child abuse centre team, with the family's agreement, through a one-way mirror. At this meeting the father acknowledged that what he had done was not right. With the support of her team, the social worker continued to work with this family. She had many anxieties about the situation, and if she had thought that Sylvie was in immediate danger, she would have taken action to protect her. But she considered that Sylvie's wish that her father should not leave, and that the family should not be broken up, had to be respected as far as was possible.

Negotiation forum

We have already argued that negotiation is a principle that should permeate the functioning of all child welfare services. Here we describe a way in which at a certain point, the principle of negotiation could be given a formal position within the structure of child welfare services.

In the current child welfare system, when parents first ask for help or willingly accept an offer of help, they enter the child welfare system and the situation can very quickly move to conflict and compulsion, without real recourse to negotiation. We argue for a negotiative intervention at just the point where the threat of compulsion can be used to give most weight to the negotiation, and conflicts can be dealt with based on the principles of trust and authority.

In many child welfare cases, somewhere along the line there will come a point when compulsion is used. For some time before compulsion is used, there will be a feeling by both the family and workers that compulsion is a future threat, and that inevitably affects people's responses. Even within the most voluntaristic services, such as drop-in centres or volunteer home visiting, there is the potential for the service provider to use some form of compulsion if the parent does not appear to be treating his or her children appropriately or is unwilling to comply with the requirements of the services. In our system there are definite points at which the compulsion (and therefore the conflict) can be ratcheted up. A professional, or group of professionals, can make a decision to use more compulsion at any of these points, but when compulsion becomes imminent enough to become threatening, the actors have entered a space of semi-compulsion.[20] This is the most productive time for negotiation because there is reason on both sides to make concessions. Final positions have not been taken and there is an incentive for change.

One of the major problems with the current system is that there is very little room for true negotiation at any of these stages. Indeed, there is often an incentive for both sides to take the conflict all the way to the formal judicial stage. From the point of view of the family it is seen as the only forum in which their story will be given equal weight, and from the professionals' point of view it is the only forum which will give them the real authority to act. In all of this the voice of the child can be completely drowned out.

The system we describe would provide an impetus for all parties to resolve conflict at the lowest level and for intervention in family life to be based on the fundamental principle of negotiation. It would put in place an authority and structure which would to allow these negotiations to happen.

It is important that this authority should not be a decision-making body, nor should it have a judicial or quasi-judicial function. Rather than addressing the question 'Is this parent providing adequate care for her child?' or 'How can she be helped/compelled to do so?', the negotiation forum provides an opportunity to address the question

'Can the professionals and the family work together, and on what basis is there a way for them to continue to do so?'

Negotiation and semi-compulsion

All child welfare systems contain elements of both voluntary engagement and compulsion, and therefore have some space where there is semi-compulsion. However, the way in which this fits into the institutional framework varies.

In France, the Children's Judge is a relatively accessible figure, working in an inquisitorial legal system with, in the children's court, a welfare discourse. Parents and children, as well as professionals, can ask for an audience with the Judge. So the journey through the child protection system appears to hurry towards compulsion because the Children's Judge is easy to access and readily used. However, the Children's Judge has to adopt a negotiative approach. She has a duty to try to find a way forward that is acceptable to the parents as well as in the interests of the child. The parents can appeal against an order if they feel that this has not been done. If they can prove that they would have agreed to a suitable alternative, the order will be overturned. (One judge commented that she and her colleagues take this possibility seriously; being a Children's Judge is only one stage in a judge's career, and successful appeals look bad on a judge's CV.) There is therefore a point in the French child welfare legal process where compulsion is not absolute, and where there is a space for negotiation.

In Flemish Belgium, where the attitude to the use of the legal system is very different, the Mediation Committee steps in before referral to the law, but when it is imminent. The very real possibility that the Mediation Committee may refer the case to the Judge means that compulsion is likely. But the intervention of the Mediation Committee provides a space for negotiation.

The Scottish Children's Hearings, as well as the Flemish Mediation Committee, both make use of lay people from the local community as arbitrators.[21] Both institutions operate at the point before compulsory powers are used.

In England, the Child Protection Conference looks at first glance as though it might provide a similar negotiative space. But in reality the procedures of the Child Protection Conference are permeated with the adversarial approach required by the legal system. An adversarial approach does not promote or facilitate negotiation. The experience of participants in the Nottingham City Negotiation Meeting (discussed later) illustrates how participation in negotiation offers different possibilities from the normal child protection procedures.

The structure of a negotiation forum

Like confidential spaces, the negotiation forum should operate in a conditional rather than absolute way. If the negotiation is not successful then the normal processes of assessment and compulsion will continue until, if necessary, the child or the perpetrator is removed from the family, or conversely the child is returned home or the perpetrator is acquitted.

This forum should not be seen as just another hurdle to cross before both parties go through the civil judicial process, nor should it be seen to be a rope for families to hang themselves on by merely providing more evidence for the authorities when the case does go to court. It would be crucial to ensure that the voice of the child is central to the proceedings, and is not an added extra.

The focus of the exercise is not information gathering or the sifting of evidence, but clarifying the perceptions of different parties about what is going wrong, and the best way forward. It is important that there should be a reliable way to follow up and monitor decisions made in the negotiation.

The exact format of the forum may vary from place to place. However, to be successful it would need to have the following characteristics:

- The negotiation forum must be an integral part of the child protection process. All cases, except real emergencies, where there is conflict between services and service users, and all cases where court proceedings are being contemplated, would use the forum.
- Children, parents, and ordinary citizens as well as social workers and other professionals must be able to approach the forum and request negotiative intervention.
- The forum must be independent of main services.
- The chairperson or facilitator should be someone with real authority in the community who commands respect from all parties.
- There should be involvement, within the process, of lay people and experts.
- The parties to the negotiation should have equivalent power.
- The remit of the forum should be very clear as should the possible outcomes of the negotiation.
- The outcome of the agreements should be monitored.

It can be seen from this list that we see the negotiation forum as informed by, but different from that of mediation in divorce or industrial disputes. The model of negotiation we are proposing draws from this tradition, but is more akin to restorative justice, which is becoming an increasingly important part of the juvenile justice system in the UK.

But negotiation should not be confined to decision-making at the semi-compulsion/compulsion interface. It should function as a principle that pervades all institutions and practices at all levels of the system.

6. The Nottingham pilot

In this section we discuss an experiment in change in child protection structures and cultures at the heart of the statutory system of working in one local authority: Nottingham City Council. Staff at all levels in the borough were interested in change, willing to take acceptable risks, but also needed the authority of their own seniors and a lengthy period of discussion and negotiation to be able to take ownership of the aims. All of this is perfectly ordinary and expectable, but equally it runs counter to contemporary policy culture which remains doggedly command and control in its approach to change.

Nottingham has had high numbers of children on the child protection register and high numbers involved in care proceedings. The management wanted to find ways of changing their responses so that fewer families were caught up in the formal child protection procedures. The aim of the project was to develop new strategies to do this, using principles derived from comparative research into European child welfare systems.

The project was initiated in the year 2000 by Children Across Europe, an informal international group of comparative child welfare researchers, and the British Association for the Study and Prevention of Child Abuse and Neglect. Some funding was provided by the National Society for the Prevention of Cruelty to Children.

A steering group was set up, made up of representatives from those organisations and from the Nottingham City Social Services

Department (SSD). The steering group appointed a half-time project manager to develop a process of change and put in place new methods of responding to local problems. The project manager knew the borough well and had previously worked in the children and families department. She was seconded to work half-time as a child protection coordinator, and combined this with the post as project manager. The steering group appointed an independent social worker as a consultant, who had training in systemic family therapy and experience in child protection. The role of the consultant was to provide the project leader with space for discussion and reflection. The project manager also had a line manager within the SSD.

The commitment of the Nottingham City SSD to the project was extremely important. The project manager provided the hands-on leadership, but she was supported by the backing of the SSD management, which enabled the field social workers and the team managers to collaborate and try out new ways of doing things. It also gave legitimacy to her work when she involved other parts of the child welfare system in the new developments.

The project's founding principles

Three developmental themes were identified by the project manager as emerging from the intercountry research. They were:

- subsidiarity – that the service should be provided and delivered at the lowest level in the heirarchy compatible with providing an effective and efficient service (see box)[22]
- support and encouragement of the professional confidence of social workers
- institutionalisation of the use of negotiation in the families' experience of child welfare services, and in the workers' approach to their task.

These three themes are a way of putting into practice the principles of trust, authority and negotiation that we have suggested. The building of professional confidence increases the ability of the workers to act with genuine authority. Negotiation is promoted by the development of subsidiarity, as well as being explicitly an aim in its own right. None of these developments can be achieved without trust between professionals as well as trust between families and professionals. At the same time, subsidiarity, confidence and negotiation help to build trust.

Subsidiarity

Subsidiarity promotes local and grass roots developments and service initiatives. It sees the provision of services by charitable bodies, religious organisations or other community-based institutions as a counterweight to control by the central state, which is regarded as distant and potentially out of touch. Through subsidiarity, in both health and welfare services, a large number of non-governmental services are involved in service delivery.

It is important to recognise that, as practised in other European countries such as Germany, the Netherlands and Belgium, the concept of subsidiarity includes an expectation that the state will provide financial support for local and non-governmental initiatives. It is also expected that the cover provided by the services should be monitored through joint committees which include governmental and non-governmental members.

Subsidiarity is not the same as the devolution of services from local government initiated in England during the 1980s. In England, many services are provided by non-government organisations, but these services are financed by the local authorities who pay the piper and call the tune. They are not financially independent; they provide the services that the local authority is prepared to pay for, and do not have the money to provide anything else.

Thus, subsidiarity is not linked to, nor associated with, non-intervention. The concept is different in important ways from the purchaser/provider split. The latter is a management strategy while subsidiarity is a political theory underpinning a definite social structure, and a philosophical statement.

How the project developed

The project leader and the consultant started with a consultation exercise that brought together social workers and other professionals closely involved in child welfare. These discussion groups were very important in helping the project leader to develop her ideas about change and new developments.

Before initiating changes, the project leader and the consultant ran a pilot training programme on reflective practice for senior practitioners and team managers. Following this they developed a basics refresher course which was offered to all of the authority's social workers in children and families teams and to family centre workers. These training developments increased receptivity to the new approaches that the further developments would promote. It was also a step towards building the workers' professional confidence.

The time taken at these stages was time well spent. It involved social workers and professionals in other child welfare services (for example, community nurses and health visitors) in developing ways of putting the principles into practice. It ensured that the ideas that underpinned the work were disseminated within the social work teams and more widely with other professionals. This work was broadly successful in creating a shared ownership of the changes that were being suggested. Building on this process, the Nottingham project developed three main strategies for change, the Child in Need meeting, the consultation forum and the negotiation meeting.

The Child in Need meeting

The most obvious point at which a family enters the child protection system is when the child is referred to an initial child protection conference (ICPC). The project found that ICPCs were often set up more readily than might really have been necessary. Social workers feel encouraged to set up an ICPC because it is a safe move; it demonstrates that they have followed procedures and protects them from criticism. As one worker put it 'people are too wary to take what I think are acceptable risks. There's a fear of being held responsible if things go wrong.'

It was also felt that other agencies would only cooperate fully if a meeting had the status of a child protection conference. Child protection conferences are the responsibility of the Area Child Protection Committee (ACPC) and they are chaired by the child protection coordinator who is employed by the ACPC; they are therefore seen as independent of the social services department, and are to some extent owned by all the agencies involved.

Borderline cases were therefore being brought into the full child protection system unnecessarily. The aim of the Nottingham strategy was to provide an alternative process that would enable a response to be made at a lower and less formal level of the system, while at the same time ensuring that a coordinated and reliable plan was made. It was decided to set up as an alternative to an ICPC, the Child in Need meeting.

This takes place when, following a Child in Need assessment, a family is seen to need multiagency support, and where there are borderline child protection concerns which may not merit registration, or where the threshold for significant harm is not met. The Child in Need meeting, like the ICPC, is chaired by the child protection coordinator, whose presence helps to raise the status of the meeting and improves the attendance and cooperation of the other agencies involved with the family.

It was also felt that social workers needed to have more space for reflection before deciding on an ICPC. It was agreed that before an ICPC is set up, the social worker and team manager must consult with the child protection coordinator. This gives the social work professionals responsible for the case the opportunity to discuss the situation with someone who is not directly involved before deciding to move into formal child protection procedures.

Other ways of coordinating support

In Germany, where there is a commitment to subsidiarity, many local child welfare services are provided by non-governmental organisations (NGOs). There is an obvious need for a meeting to coordinate the various services provided by NGOs and the local authority social service for children and families, the Jugendamt.

The *Hilfeplangespräch* (help plan meeting) is a statutory requirement and is held to coordinate action at the point where the family's complex needs are seen to require the help of several agencies. The aim is to agree an assessment of the problem and set up a coordinated plan of help between the family and the agencies. The meetings are attended by the family and by any social workers or other professionals involved.

There are similarities with the Nottingham Child in Need meeting. Both involve the family, the child welfare department and workers from a range of agencies. Both aim to coordinate a package of help and support involving some local authority funding.

However, although the Child in Need meeting provides a way of avoiding the child protection process for some, it is nevertheless a step on the route that can end in court. The *Hilfeplangespräch* is not linked to child protection procedures. It Is not institutionally connected to the court process. The *Jugendamt* can refer cases to the Judge for Children and works with the courts, but they have no equivalent to the child protection conference. The *Hilfeplangespräch* is not, as is the Child in Need meeting, an alternative to something more formal. It exists in its own right.

Negotiation is central to the work of a *Hilfeplangespräch*. One writer comments that where the members of the meeting do not have the skills or the time to work in this way, the process becomes 'a bureaucratic requirement … and its potential opportunities are squandered'.

These small changes have been effective in shifting the balance of the process towards the support of families. They have prevented referrals into the initial child protection conference process and enabled more work to be done in cooperation with families, and with improved cooperation and coordination between services.

The development of the Child in Need meeting supports the principles identified by the project leader. It promotes the use of the lowest level of formal intervention possible and encourages reflective practice. The Child in Need meeting also promotes a more negotiative approach than a child protection conference.

It is interesting that the child protection coordinator, who is identified with the ACPC, rather than with the social work department, had to be used both to support the confidence of the social workers and to influence the response of other agencies. This suggests that the status of social workers and social services departments is low, both in their own eyes and in the eyes of other professionals. It also suggests that more use could be made of the strength of the ACPC as an interagency and interdisciplinary body in promoting a more integrated approach to work with children and families.

The consultation forum

The second strategy, the consultation forum, was targeted specifically at building the confidence of social workers in their professional roles and skills.

Social workers and their managers are responsible for managing high-risk, complex cases. They are faced with the conflicting interests of different family members in relation to a wide range of needs. The work requires reflection, discussion and the ability to cooperate and coordinate action with a wide range of other agencies and professions. With current pressures on social workers and their managers, time for discussion and reflection is hard to achieve. The end result is that some workers' use of professional judgement is limited and they struggle to act with confidence and authority.

The consultation forum aims to encourage the development of reflective practice, a mode of work in which practitioners stand back from their day-to-day experience of the task and try to see how their intervention is affecting the way that the family functions. They are observing change in the family, evaluating the way in which change has come about, and their part in it. An assessment of a family will be the starting point of their work, but what is crucial is how the family reacts to this intervention. Depending on the response of the family, an adjustment might be needed to the assessment, and therefore to the way that the social worker goes about her task. The practitioner is a part of the system with which she is working, but must retain independence of thought and judgement in relation to it. This movement between connectedness and separateness is achieved through the capacity to reflect on one's own contribution to the evolution of the system through time.

Reflective practice is not easy, and workers need the support of their institution to try to work that way. They need the type of supervision that will encourage them to confront their own difficulties and think through the implications of their observations and their assessments.

To meet the need for this kind of supervision, the consultation forum was set up to provide staff with the opportunity to bring cases to a multiagency group for discussion. The forum has a group of core members, one of whom must be a social services Service Manager, which gives the meeting departmental authority. The forum accepts responsibility for the advice and guidance that it gives which allows workers to feel supported; responsibility is not located solely with an individual worker and team manager. The forum can call on a pool of multiagency personnel, who can be invited to the meeting depending on the issues involved in each particular case and can give expert advice on, for example, domestic violence, mental health issues or drug and alcohol misuse. Bringing such cases to the forum, with relevant multiagency staff, gives staff the opportunity to reflect on alternative approaches. Expertise and knowledge can be shared, increasing the professional confidence and autonomy of the social workers. Increased confidence enables workers to challenge the procedures culture that dominates social work practice and leads to overuse of formal child protection measures. The forum helps the individual workers to develop their professional skills. It supports their professional confidence, increasing their professional judgement and competence.

The negotiation meeting

One of the aims of the Nottingham project was to encourage the use of negotiation as a standard approach to working in most circumstances. The specific aim of the negotiation neeting is to avoid the use of compulsory powers by acting as a buffer or filter before the use of legal intervention into family life.

Independent professionals, who are not employed by the social services department, chair the negotiation meeting. Two workers were recruited to act as chair, one seconded for one half-day a week by the local Family Mediation Service, the other a manager from a local *Sure Start* scheme. Both workers have experience in family support and child protection. Although the process of the meeting cannot be regarded purely as mediation, the principles of mediation are very important to the way it is run.

A social worker who feels that she is not making any progress in her work with a family, and is anxious about the risks to the children, can ask for a negotiation meeting to be set up. The aim of the negotiation meeting is to hear the views of the main parties involved, to attempt to broker an agreement and avoid the use of care proceedings. The family is free to refuse to take part in the meeting, but if the family agrees, the two mediators first meet with them to ascertain how they view the situation and why they think that things have become stuck. The mediators also seek to find out how the family feels that communication could be improved and how they might be helped to work together with the social services to try to avoid more intrusive intervention into their family life.

The mediators then meet with the social worker and the team manager. They again seek to identify what are the blocks or barriers to working effectively with the family. Following this, the negotiation meeting is set up. Both parties attend the meeting and the mediators aim to promote a better understanding on the part of the family and of the social worker about each other's hopes, needs and anxieties. The mediators try to help them to arrive at a voluntary agreement and clarify what the social services might do if the situation fails to improve and concerns remain about a child's welfare.

This is the extent of their role, and they have no decision-making powers.

If referrals to the negotiation meeting increase, and it is adopted as part of the system, it is planned that parents should also be able to ask for a meeting. Written and verbal information about the meetings would be given to all service users.

The Nottingham negotiation meeting has so far had only one referral, but the outcome of that referral was strikingly positive. A parent was at loggerheads with the social services department, and was always out when the social worker called. Her child was neglected and missing a great deal of school. An arrangement for occasional respite foster care was not working, and the only way forward was to apply for a care order. As a result of the negotiation meeting, the mother overcame her fear of the department and began to cooperate actively and enthusiastically with her social worker. Her child's school attendance improved and a plan was agreed for the use of respite foster care if necessary.

Good communication was established with other agencies involved with the family. The mother's comment after the meeting was: 'it's the first time I have felt that anyone has really listened to me'. In avoiding the costs of one court hearing, the borough has saved enough to fund the operation of the negotiation meeting several times over.

Overview of the project

As with all such ventures, the progress of the project is affected by events in other parts of the system. The department has been undergoing a major restructuring programme, and as a result the introduction of the negotiation meeting was slightly delayed, so there has been less experience of its use than there could have been. In spite of the restructuring, the Child in Need meeting has become part of the local procedures and the department is supporting the continuation of the consultation forum. The changes have the support of departmental staff and are popular with the social workers.

The Nottingham project demonstrates that there is a range of ways in which our three principles of trust, authority and negotiation can be promoted. The Child in Need meeting increases the opportunities for social workers to build trust with families, by offering support without the stigma and blame attached to the ICPC and registration. It increases interaction with other professionals at the stage when there is an expectation of positive outcome. This leads to an increase in trust between professionals.

The consultation forum is an interesting and imaginative way of providing the quality of supervision that we think is needed to develop the professional authority of social workers. It provides support, space for reflection and the stimulus and challenge of an interdisciplinary approach. Through the involvement of a multiagency and multidisciplinary membership, the consultation forum has also led to an improvement in interagency understanding and cooperation.

The structure of the negotiation meeting is very similar to the negotiation forum described earlier in this chapter. As well as providing the means for the use of negotiation in a formalised way, it is a means of increasing and institutionalising the role of negotiation. Of the three developments in the Nottingham project, the negotiation meeting is the one that has required the most faith on the part of the SSD. At the same time, it is the innovation that has produced the most direct saving in social work time and expenditure on legal processes.

The process of change

The details of the new developments in Nottingham City are very interesting and encouraging in their own right, but equally important is the process that enabled the changes to be made.

Cultural change and structural change went hand-in-hand as part of the same process. Leadership and ideas were provided at all levels of the system. The specific changes made to the Nottingham City child protection procedures might or might not be relevant and useful in other places, but the process by which the developments were devised and initiated was integral to its success.

This process cannot be rushed.[23] A patient process of consultation using focus groups was undertaken, which gave workers in social services and other agencies the opportunity to learn about each other and develop trust. This led, on the one hand, to the introduction of cultural change through social work staff training that promoted reflective practice; and on the other, to the setting up of the Child in Need meetings and the consultation forum. Both the Child in Need meeting and the consultation forum involve workers from other agencies and depend on their active participation. The Nottingham developments could not have taken place without interagency and interdisciplinary cooperation that took place in a constructive atmosphere of genuine debate.

An important aspect of these developments was the leadership provided by the steering group and the management of the Nottingham City SSD. Although the immediate leadership for the development of change took place at a middle management level, the will to make changes was validated and endorsed by the top management. At the same time, the social workers in the field were drawn into the process and played an important part in defining the changes that were needed and developing the ways that they could be realised. A great deal was down to the leadership of the project manager, but without reliable support from the higher levels of the organisation, she would have been greatly handicapped. The provision of an external consultant for the project, who gave the project leader a space for reflection, illustrates the role of supervision.

The Nottingham project illustrates firstly that important changes can be made at the local level, and secondly how changes in culture and changes in structure need to work together.

7. The way ahead: developing a new system

If it is accepted that there is a crisis in the way the state delivers welfare services to families, then something has to change.

Taken together, the principles of trust, authority and negotiation constitute the basis for a new and radical concept of public service provision, rooted in a respect for the rights of adults and children to exercise the maximum feasible autonomy over their own affairs, even in circumstances of acute interpersonal conflict and risk. The use of these principles requires professionals to think in new ways, which neither hand over power to users in an unrealistic manner, abrogating their own authority, nor revert to old fashioned paternalism. These principles organise relationships at the difficult boundary between the law, the state and the family in a manner which accepts rather than avoids the fact that this is a conflicted terrain. They recognise that tensions in these relationships are necessary and usually manageable.

Much of the time current practice in child welfare and protection tries and succeeds in using some or all of these principles. But this largely happens despite, rather than because of, the overall principles shaping the operation of the system. Space for thinking, negotiating, taking risks, or working in confidence has to be fought for and won at local level, rather than being taken for granted as the organising ethos of the work, supported by institutions which legitimate it.

Social services and other agencies serving children and families have gone through enormous upheavals in the past decade, and we hesitate to recommend another revolution which potentially could disrupt services even further. It is also true that low morale and poor training are major challenges facing today's child protection system, and that another major shake up will simply add to these problems, causing child protection workers to feel de-skilled and powerless. Nevertheless, given the direction of government policy, large-scale structural changes are very likely anyway. At the very least, there are going to be many more multidisciplinary teams, multiagency and colocated services and virtual teams. While there are bound to be some difficulties in interdisciplinary work, the potential gains are enormous. We welcome these developments, but believe that they can only succeed if they adhere to the three principles.

We have argued that all the changes over the past 15 years have led towards increased bureaucracy and regulation, and that this has been a dead end. If there is to be change it must get us out of the blind alley of checklist practice and into authoritative professionalism which involves trust between the public, professionals and policy-makers. This trust must be mutually earned; it cannot be decreed or simply wished for, and it is not only about the media image of professionals. Building trust between professionals, and between professionals and the public, will be a slow and painstaking process and there are no quick fixes.

This document has set out the principles on which change can be based and put forward some ways of implementing those principles. The small-scale developments in Nottingham are an example of how bottom-up developments can begin to change the way professionals work with each other. If these sorts of changes were repeated across the country this could be the beginning of the radical changes which are ultimately needed.

Any change in function or structure is accompanied by a degree of risk, and the changes advocated here are certainly not risk-free. The biggest risk is that the easily achieved structural changes are made, but not the more painstaking changes to the way professionals view the task. It would be tragic if confidential services were developed only to be subject to the same regulation, performance targets, poor resourcing and defensive practice which dog the current system. If new structures are simply reflections of the current cultures then change will not be worth while.

One safeguard against the dangers of precipitating structural change is that the changes should not, and in some cases cannot, be implemented overnight. Instead, a policy for engaging professionals and community members in the process of developing new ways forward should now be developed, and new forms of service delivery should emerge based on the template for a system set out above. Only in this way will the new system gain the public legitimacy, the involvement of community members and the support of professionals that the current system so clearly lacks.

Trust, authority and negotiation: recommendations for change

It will not be possible to develop a single, coherent child protection/child welfare system which can address the whole range of issues facing children. No one structure is going to solve all the problems. This is not only because of the diversity of types of problems but also because the system itself has conflicting objectives: it has to protect children while engaging and supporting parents and siblings; it has to maintain confidentiality while sharing information where relevant; it has to target the most at risk while providing universal services for all.

The fundamental changes we would like to see are:

- increased professional authority and autonomy
- increased accountability for individuals and teams
- formal and informal forums for professionals and practitioners to take a step back, and reflect on and discuss difficult cases and situations
- greater involvement of communities in management and decisions
- diversity of forms of delivery of welfare and points of access to the system for children and families.

These things have traditionally been seen as in opposition. Professional authority is often viewed as the opposite of community involvement and autonomy is seen as the opposite of accountability, but these are false dichotomies. The public tends to trust professionals who are seen as powerful, but also accountable. Most people believe that it is much easier to negotiate with authoritative practitioners than with a faceless organisation.[24] Workers who have more authority and autonomy will, we believe, tend to feel more committed and satisfied in their work, despite the higher levels of personal accountability we are proposing: an increase in job satisfaction which may well help to solve the recruitment crisis that is currently crippling child welfare and social care as a whole.

Interestingly, government policy is in some ways moving in this direction. The freedoms and flexibilities given to well performing councils under the Comprehensive Performance Assessment and the establishment of foundation hospitals express the belief that if you are doing well you should be less regulated. This should apply to individual practitioners as well as agencies and public services.

Structural changes

There is not one magic structural solution to the current problems in child protection and public services generally. But by encouraging diversity within an overall framework progress can be made. There are a number of developments which could be piloted on a local or national level.

- We would support a large-scale relocation of social workers from town halls to multidisciplinary teams based in schools, health centres and the community. While social services departments were an important development in the history of welfare provision, they have become monolithic and defensive organisations, constantly struggling with thresholds and struggling to work with other professional groups. In Europe many of these issues are less severe, partly because social workers and other social services staff usually work in multidisciplinary teams which are frequently physically located in multiagency teams linked to schools, health centres and community organisations. We believe that such a move will allow social welfare and child protection to reach out to the community and will greatly increase the possibilities for trust, authority and negotiation.[25]

- This in turn would create multiple access points to the system which would encourage self-referral and engagement. Familiarity with and exposure to child welfare professionals would allow children, families and communities to engage in a dialogue with professionals about their roles and responsibilities. We strongly believe that some of these access points should provide the possibility of high levels of confidentiality for children and parents so that they can talk about their problems without the necessity of immediate statutory intervention.
- Social workers and other child welfare professionals should be treated as individuals who are part of a team but responsible for their own work, rather like GPs. Social workers and GPs have been at extreme ends of a continuum, with GPs acting almost entirely autonomously, while social workers are part of a hierarchical and bureaucratic structure. With the advent of Primary Care Trusts, GPs are now being required to work much more as part of a team; conversely, we think that social workers should be given more professional autonomy.
- The corollary to this is that social workers should be provided with non-managerial supervision focused on the complex and subtle dynamics of work with children and families. It is unlikely that, in the current climate, social workers will be enabled to work outside of a management structure (as GPs do). But the extent to

which management has taken over the organisation of professional responses needs to be severely curtailed.

- Trained mediators should become part of the system, intervening in all cases where there is conflict within the system. This would include interagency conflict, user–professional and user–user conflict. Our experience in Nottingham and research in Europe indicate that mediation is most likely to work if it is, more or less, a requirement. So the system needs to build in mediation. Mediation should become a normal requirement where cases are going to court or children are being placed on the Child Protection Register, as well as a voluntary exercise for those workers and families who are struggling with conflict. In the current system there is little incentive for families or workers to resort to mediation, and the risks for both sides are high.
- ACPCs need to be given statutory powers. They already (as the Nottingham experience demonstrates) have the capability to provide interdisciplinary and interagency authority. This needs to be supported by increased community involvement.
- A change in the adversarial legal system in child and family law towards a restorative system would be an enormous encouragement to cultural change throughout the child welfare system. There has been a huge growth of interest in the Restorative Justice approaches to offending, especially of young offenders. This approach has not yet reached the child protection process, but has great potential in this area. The influence of the adversarial legal system on the child protection system is pervasive, and is one foundation of the culture of blame in the system.[26] Many of the kinds of changes that we would like to promote would be easier if we did not have an adversarial legal system. We acknowledge that major changes to the legal system seem unlikely, but the changes

> in the field of youth offenders suggest that there may be some scope for adjustment.

Some of these changes are being actively promoted elsewhere, and are quite likely to happen, while some are more contentious. While we believe their implementation would make an enormous difference to professional practice and to children and families, they could be implemented without major disruption to current structures.

Such structural changes would facilitate the use of the principles of trust, authority and negotiation. Structural change has its place, and the structural changes outlined above are ones that we would very much like to see. But to work, even these changes depend on cultural change. Engagement with cultural change needs to be made at every level, from the policy-makers of central government to the managers in child welfare services and the individual professional in the field.

There is too much at stake for children, parents and society as a whole, for us to do nothing. We have the understanding needed to succeed. Lasting reform requires political will, professional courage and intellectual clarity.

Annex 1: Recent government policies and initiatives for children[27]

Active Community Programme

To pilot new and imaginative ways of demonstrating a step change in public involvement in the community and to test out a wide range of approaches to increasing and diversifying public involvement in community life.

Behaviour and Attendance Package

Range of services including Behaviour and Education Support Teams, Safer Schools Partnerships, Truancy Sweeps, Extended Schools, etc, aimed at improving behaviour, reducing truancy and exclusion and addressing emotional problems of children in school.

Children's Centres

Commitment to create multidisciplinary centres for childcare, family support and other services in the 20% most deprived wards in England.

Children's Fund

To help tackle child poverty and social exclusion. The Fund is focused on children aged 5–13 years and is given to every local authority in England based on the number of children in poverty in that area.

Children's Trusts

Pilot of initiatives to pool budgets and join services between health, education, social services and other relevant agencies.

Communities Against Drugs

To provide funding to local communities to support interventions that: disrupt local drugs markets by tackling both the supply and demand; tackle drug-related crime; and address associated anti-social behaviour.

Community Empowerment Fund

To support community and voluntary sector involvement in Local Strategic Partnerships.

Connexions

Universal initiative for 14–19-year-olds which aims to provide every young person with advice on education and employment. Children and young people are provided with a range of information services including personal advisers.

Creative Partnerships

Works to give school children in disadvantaged areas throughout England the opportunity to develop their potential, their ambition, their creativity and imagination through sustainable partnerships with creative and cultural organisations, businesses and individuals.

Drug Action Teams

To deliver the government's national drugs strategy at a local level.

Early Excellence Centres

To develop, demonstrate and disseminate models of excellence in the delivery of centre-based integrated multiagency services, which meet the needs of children and families, raise standards and achieve national impact. Centres are expected to offer high quality integrated early years education and care, family support and training.

Education Action Zones

To raise educational standards through partnerships with local businesses, parents and the community, developing new skills, experience and innovative solutions to overcome local barriers to achievement.

Excellence in Cities

To drive up standards in schools in the major cities, higher and faster, to match the standards of excellence found in our best schools, so that city parents and city children expect and gain as much from their schools as their counterparts anywhere else in the country.

Health Action Zones

To target a special effort on a number of areas where the health of local people can be improved by better integrated arrangements for treatment and care.

Healthy Living Centres

To fund centres promoting health and well-being, accessible to 20% of the population of the UK, targeted at the most deprived communities.

Healthy Schools Programme

To create a healthy ethos within schools, improve the health and self-esteem of the school community; and enable children to make healthier choices and improve their educational achievement.

Local Preventative Strategy

Requirement that every local authority should have a strategy to prevent social exclusion and promote positive outcomes for children at risk.

National Service Framework for Children

Set of standards which health, social services and related agencies will be required to adhere to when delivering services to children, families and parents-to-be.

Neighbourhood Learning Centres

To ensure that people in disadvantaged areas have access to the education and training they need.

Neighbourhood Nursery Centres

To provide affordable, accessible, quality childcare in the most disadvantaged areas.

Neighbourhood Renewal Fund

Aims to enable the 88 most deprived local authorities to improve services, narrowing the gap between deprived areas and the rest of England.

Neighbourhood Support Fund

To re-engage the most disaffected and disengaged 13–19-year-olds, living in some of the most deprived areas, back into education, training and employment.

New Deal for Communities

To tackle multiple deprivation in the poorest areas, taking forward the government's commitment to combat social exclusion.

Overarching Strategy for Children

Government's commitment to all children. Consists of a set of core principles for all services, plus a set of outcomes for children which the government will aim to achieve.

Partnership Development Fund

To help build the capacity of local Crime and Disorder Reduction Partnerships to deliver reductions in crime and disorder and enhance partnership working in their area.

Parenting Fund

Announced in 2002, will provide parent training and support to parents from disadvantaged and socially excluded families.

Positive Futures

To use sport to reduce anti-social behaviour, crime and drug misuse among 10–16-year-olds from disadvantaged estates and neighbourhoods.

Safer Communities Initiative

To provide extra resources to help local crime-reduction partnerships to tackle crime locally.

Single Regeneration Budget

To enhance the quality of life of local people in areas of need by reducing the gap between deprived and other areas, and between different groups.

Spaces for Sport and Arts

To build links between schools and communities and to encourage social inclusion in areas of multiple deprivation through improving the quality and quantity of facilities for sport and arts in primary schools.

Sports Action Zones

To help bring the benefits of sport to deprived communities.

Sure Start

Sure Start Local Programmes are the cornerstone of the government's drive to tackle child poverty and social exclusion. It works with parents-to-be, parents and children to promote the physical, intellectual and social development of babies and young children under four. They are concentrated in neighbourhoods where a high proportion of children are living in poverty and where Sure Start can help them succeed by pioneering new ways of working to improve services.

Sure Start Plus

To reduce the risk of long-term social exclusion and poverty from teenage pregnancy.

Youth Inclusion Programme

To prevent re-offending by working with up to 50 of the 13–16-year-olds most at risk of being drawn into crime in the local area.

Youth Music Action Zones

To give children and young people in areas with least access to music-making, the chance to get involved in a range of musical activities.

Annex 2: Child protection systems and systems theory

It is necessary to set out some of the basic concepts of systems in child protection on which our argument is based. The main theoretical basis for our argument is provided by complex, or open, systems theory, and by the ecological model.[28] This approach is becoming increasingly important in contemporary understandings of policy and practice in human services. The open systems model is a development from the closed or hard systems approach which envisages human systems as analogous to mechanical or software systems. All systems theory is underpinned by the following basic concepts:

Emergence At its most basic, emergence means that the whole is greater than the sum of its parts. In mechanical systems this means that, for example, a pile of motor engine components cannot drive a car, but put together so that they interact in the correct way and with the right conditions (enough petrol to run, the right temperature) the engine will run a car. In organic and social systems, when the interaction of basic components reaches a particular degree of complexity, then qualitatively new properties may suddenly emerge. In turn these may now act upon the basic elements, and the relationship of whole to part is one of true interdependence.

Interdependence Changes in one part of the system will affect the system as a whole. Systems are often characterised as interlocking networks or flow diagrams that show that even small changes in one part will affect the whole. For example, an injury to the knee can cause pain in the shoulder or back as strain is put on muscles not directly involved in the injury.

Adaptation All systems change in response to their context: systems interact with other systems and adapt to their environment. For example, relationships between family members may be profoundly changed if the family moves to another city, or the father is made redundant.

The special nature of complex adaptive systems

Closed systems Closed systems are characterised by definable inputs, processes, outputs and outcomes. The model is based on the notions of homeostasis and equilibrium, in which action by the system involves either adaptation to or accommodation of the environment.[29] In theorising policy development, closed systems theory still lends itself to a command and control model, where the policy-maker can change developments on-the-ground in predictable ways with carefully considered laws and guidance.

Open systems In the past two decades there have been developments in systemic theorising which have moved beyond this model towards the open or complex systems approach. According to this way of thinking, most biological and social systems are not driven by equilibrium, but rather by complex and constant change. Interventions at any point in the system will create consequences, but these are not easily predictable from the initial parameters of the system, and are not necessarily proportionate to the input itself. The analogy often used to evoke this process is the butterfly flapping its wings in Tokyo causing a hurricane in Texas.

In effect, this model asserts that chance events can magnify the effects of small inputs into the system, and can diminish the effects of large inputs. Some policy-makers accept this view, but still believe that the system can be controlled. They believe it is possible to engineer the system so that the butterfly flaps its wings in a way that causes the hurricane the policy-maker wishes to create. However, complexity theory suggests that this is not possible, even in principle.

It is important to recognise that this way of thinking does not imply that all outcomes are random, nor that all processes are unmanageable. What an open systems perspective does is to show that processes are never entirely controllable or predictable, and that there are theoretical limits to our understanding of these processes. Factors far outside the control of policy-makers and practitioners will intervene to affect the services. On a psychological level this means living with uncertainty and accepting that uncertainty is fundamental to policy management and practice in child welfare.[30]

Different levels of or within systems

Systems such as child protection act at different levels: practice management, policy and government. Children also live within different systems: the family, community and the nation.[31] Each interaction between a professional and a child or family is informed by all these levels. This book is fundamentally concerned with what actually goes on between practitioners, children and families, but recognises that this encounter is complex, and is influenced by many factors.

Change happens at all levels and changes in one level can affect other levels. Real change must occur at all levels of the system. Changes that are only made at one level are very much less likely to have major impacts on other levels. Changes at one level are often resisted at other levels, so that changes in policy, for example, do not necessarily lead to changes in practice.

Fluid boundaries

One aspect of complex adaptive systems is that, unlike closed systems, they do not have easily definable boundaries. Virtually all systems, including hard systems such as machines, trees or the solar system, have grey areas on the margins where there can be arguments about whether this or that aspect is really part of the system. But open systems are by definition fluid and subject to different definitions depending on location in relation to the system. This applies particularly to large-scale systems such as the legal system and the transport system, but also to small-scale human systems such as a family or a school.

The child protection and child welfare systems, therefore, are not definable in a unique way and may include different aspects depending on the perspective of the discussion. Narrow definitions of the child protection system, for example, will include the people, processes and systems for investigating complaints about individuals alleged to have abused children, and the assessment and interventions which follow investigation. But in some contexts the system will include the efforts made by government departments and agencies to prevent abuse and other negative outcomes for children. The widest definitions will include issues to do with community structures, wider policies to do with children such as the availability of childcare or the maintenance of parks and efforts to reduce poverty and social exclusion. In this pamphlet we generally use the shorthand of 'the child protection system' to include all those efforts by professionals and volunteers to safeguard the welfare of individual children, but we do not attempt to define exactly the parameters of the system.

Conflict and power relationships

The closed system model does not attempt to address conflict as an issue in understanding systems, because it is based on an implicit assumption that conflict and tension are disruptions to the system. Normally it is assumed that the system operates to resolve conflict and recreate equilibrium. Conflict, tension and compulsion are seen as matters to be avoided. Much thinking about child welfare is at least implicitly based on this world view. Welfare is seen as part of a virtuous circle in which the state intervenes to empower citizens to take control of their own lives. Users then deploy their skills for the benefit of their children and their local community. The managerialist approach is a variation of this because it poses problems in the system as being primarily technical rather than addressing real conflicts of interest between different stakeholders. This assumes that more efficient, effective and economic services are beneficial to all stakeholders, and therefore the main challenge is to put in place systems that can achieve these ends.

In contrast, in an open system model, conflict and tension can be regarded as essential components and although conflict is disruptive, it is also creative and dynamic. This view recognises and accepts the need be receptive to recurring tension. In resolving one conflict another may be generated but this may be productive. These sorts of conflicts are inescapable in any process which involves social change, at the micro or the macro level. There are very few interventions which are entirely win–win and most social processes create losers as well as winners.

Related to conflict is the exercise of power. Because of its basic philosophy of inclusion and consensus, discussions of welfare tend to underplay power relationships or to see them as problematic and dangerous. The whole partnership practice movement is an attempt to address the problem of conflict, but it often seems like an effort to avoid conflict rather than work with it. Conflict operates at every level of the system: within individual cases, local management, national policy and the wider society and culture.

Within child welfare the core conflict or tension is the degree to which provision of services can be voluntaristic and consensual, rather than compulsory and mandatory. We argue that conflict is implicit in all welfare provision, but so is support and help. Conflict can be productive as well as destructive, and we argue that conflict and tension can be harnessed to better help and protect children and families. There are other, equally important tensions that underlie all child welfare policies. These include tensions between centralisation and local variation, prevention and crisis intervention, child focus and family focus, targeting and universality. These tensions are inherent in any policy area, but are particularly acute in child protection. They should not be ignored or denied; they have the potential to create a dialectic out of which positive change can develop.

Unintended consequences

Because open systems are complex, changes will inevitably produce outcomes which are not predictable. It is not possible to foresee all the consequences of interventions or policies, and the social policy field is littered with examples of unintended consequences.[32] One particular area of policy dogged by unintended consequences is that of performance indicators and league tables. This is because although indicators or targets are intended to measure a whole range of behaviours, they have a reflexive effect so that behaviour becomes defined by the target rather than by the underlying process that the target is supposed to be measuring. The classic example of this is the attempt to reduce waiting lists for hospital surgery, which has resulted in less urgent cases being prioritised because they can be dealt with quicker.

In child protection there have been many examples of policies which have produced perverse outcomes. In the mid-1990s the whole structure of the education system changed, so that schools had much more autonomy and the role of the LEA was considerably reduced. This was an attempt to improve choice and educational attainment. However, it had a negative impact on the child protection system in that strategically it became very difficult to manage child protection work in schools. Each school individually had to sign up to child protection policies, and the representation of Education on Area Child Protection Committees (ACPCs) became very problematic.[33]

Achieving change in systems

All interactions between professionals and the public are informed by 'cultures'. National culture informs not only the way the job is done by professionals, but also the expectations which children and families have of services. Professional culture is also important. However, professional culture may not be in synch with the culture of the local community, and professional cultures themselves vary. Different professions within the child welfare field may approach similar problems differently.

These factors affect the actual situation between the individual practitioner and the child or family in each case. Ultimately they are about the relationship between the child, the family and the state. There may be conflict within or between these different spheres, and professional culture may be at odds with government policy or management culture. Professionals are not simply representatives of the state or of their agencies, nor are they simply individuals operating according to their own judgement. Professional practice is a complex amalgam of different cultural and organisational inputs. Professional practice in child welfare is not necessarily resistant to change as such, but may be very resistant to changes that go against its professional culture.

One example of major systemic changes in the child welfare field was the very rapid adoption of managerialist approaches in the early 1980s. In the 1970s practitioners generally had no idea at all what their services cost or what outcomes they produced, and even managers had very little financial or statistical information to rely on. By the end of the 1980s there had been a change in the zeitgeist in public sector management due to Thatcherite polices. Structural changes such as purchaser/provider splits and improvements in technology had created an utterly transformed management environment in which professional knowledge was considered a liability and managers relied heavily on information and generic management theories. Practitioners became aware of the cost of their interventions, the core business of their service and the mission of their agency. Processes became much more regulated and managed.

However, systems also have a tendency to resist change. This is because systems operate according to an often unacknowledged premise which is usually in conflict with the official policy of the organisation. While that logic persists the basic function of the system is likely to be constant despite structural changes.

The combinations of these factors are very frustrating to policy-makers who are intent on instituting step changes in systems. The ongoing debate about the NHS is an example of a system which has been subjected to constant major structural change over many years, but still looks to politicians as if it is 'stuck' in its old ways of doing things and ripe for yet more 'radical' change.

We argue that another change in the zeitgeist is needed which will underpin the changes in the system we advocate, but we recognise the difficulties which policy-makers must confront to introduce significant changes in practice.

Notes

1 Cawson P, Wattam C, Brooker S and Kelly G, *Child Maltreatment in the United Kingdom: a Study of the Prevalence of Abuse and Neglect* (London: NSPCC, 2000).

2 This handbook, published by the Department of Health in 2001, provides an assessment tool for social workers and other professionals. All children who need, or may be found to need, services of family support are to be assessed according to this manual. The *Framework* gives a detailed outline of the methodology of the assessment process and provides a statement of the theories that underlie the method and the supporting research. It includes forms that should be completed as part of the assessment and sets out a time scale within which the assessment should take place.

3 Hetherington et al, for example, found that if a parent has a mental health problem, virtually all the professional attention is focused on this issue rather than on the needs or perspectives of the children in their own right. Hetherington R, Baistow K, Katz K, Mesie J and Trowell J, *The Welfare of Children with Mentally Ill Parents: learning from inter-country comparisons* (Chichester: John Wiley, 2001).

4 See Cooper A, Hetherington R, Baistow K, Pitts J and Spriggs A, *Positive Child Protection: a view from abroad* (Lyme Regis: Russell House Publishing, 1995) and Hetherington R, Cooper A, Smith P and Wilford G, *Protecting Children: messages from Europe* (Lyme Regis: Russell House Publishing, 1997), for detailed descriptions of these services.

5 *Kinder und Jugendhilfegesitz*, 1990 para 8, sect 3.

6 The Icarus Project took place from 1997 to 2000. See Hetherington R, Baistow K, Johanson J and Mesie J, *Professional Interventions for Mentally Ill Parents and their Children: building a European model. Final Report on the Icarus Project* (London: Brunel University, Centre for Comparative Social Work Studies, 2000) and

Hetherington et al, *The Welfare of Children with Mentally Ill Parents.*

7 *Framework for the Assessment of Children in Need and their Families* (London: Department of Health, 2001).

8 see *Working Together to Safeguard Children* (London: Department of Health, 1999).

9 *Serving Children Well; a new vision for children's services* (London: Local Government Association, 2002).

10 Examples are taken from a research project into the experiences of parents of the child welfare services of France, Germany and England, which took place between 1996 and 1998. There were two reports: Wilford G, *Families Ask for Help* (London: Brunel University, Centre for Comparative Social Work Studies, 1997) and Baistow K, Hetherington R, Spriggs A and Yelloly M, *Parents Speaking: Anglo-French perceptions of child welfare interventions* (London: Brunel University, Centre for Comparative Social Work Studies, 1998).

11 Bell L and Tooman P, 'Mandatory reporting laws: a critical overview', *International Journal of Law and the Family* 8, 3 (1994): 337–56. Kalichman S, Craig M, and Follingstad D, 'Professionals' adherence to mandatory child abuse reporting laws: effects of responsibility attribution, confidence ratings, and situational factors', *Child Abuse and Neglect* 14, 1 (1990): 69–77.

12 Hallett C and Birchall E, *Coordination and Child Protection: a review of the literature* (Edinburgh: HMSO, 1992).

13 The researchers used the professionally accepted definitions of abuse. The study showed that about three times as many children were defined as having been abused using professional definitions, as those victims defining themselves as having been abused. For sexual abuse the figures are 19% and 6% respectively. Cawson P, Wattam C, Brooker S and Kelly G, *Child Maltreatment in the United Kingdom: a study of the prevalence of child abuse and neglect* (London: NSPCC, 2000).

14 Pringle K, *Children and Social Welfare in Europe* (Buckingham : Open University Press, 1998).

15 see Cooper A, Hetherington R, Baistow K, Pitts J and Spriggs A, *Positive Child Protection: a view from abroad* (Lyme Regis: Russell House Publishing, 1995).

16 Any reference to Belgium and child protection or child abuse raises questions about the Dutroux case. This was a notorious and tragic case where children were sexually abused and murdered by a paedophile, someone from outside their family and unknown to them. It raised serious questions about the efficiency and conduct of the police, and there were massive protest demonstrations in Brussels. The child protection system was reviewed after this and the possibility of introducing mandatory reporting was debated extensively at government and local levels in the Flemish community. A decision was taken not to introduce mandatory reporting on the grounds that this

would discourage abusing parents who might otherwise ask for help.

17 see Hetherington R, Cooper A, Smith P and Wilford G, *Protecting Children: messages from Europe* (Lyme Regis: Russell House Publishing, 1997).

18 Beck U, *Risk Society: towards a new modernity* (London: Sage, 1992), p75.

19 Dingwall R, Eekelaar J, and Murray T, *The Protection of Children: state intervention and family life*, 2nd edn (Aldershot: Avebury, 1995).

20 Hetherington R, Cooper A, Smith P and Wilford G, *Protecting Children: messages from Europe* (Lyme Regis: Russel House Publishing, 1997).

21 for more information on both these institutions see Hetherington R, Cooper A, Smith P and Wilford G, *Protecting Children: messages from Europe* (Lyme Regis: Russel House Publishing, 1997).

22 see Schäfer H, 'Legal Notebook: the principle of subsidiarity', *Social Work in Europe* 2, 3 (1995): 52–3.

23 The first discussions took place in 2000, and the project started in January 2001. The funding will come to an end in June 2003.

24 Anfilogof (2002) conducted focus groups with carers and found that social workers lacked autonomy, were frustrated when workers had to ask managers about minor issues and could not understand why individual workers could not make even minor decisions. Anfilogof S, *Focus on the Future – key messages from focus groups about the future of social work training* (London: Department of Health, 2002).

25 The location of social workers in schools is already happening in a piecemeal way. A school in Manchester has had a social worker in place for the last few years, and has found that this has had many benefits. There are some practical difficulties to be overcome. Multidisciplinary work initially gave rise to some problems over confidentiality but these were resolved. And as the school has a large catchment area, there have also been problems over differing geographical boundaries between different services. But none of the difficulties have been unmanageable. The project is backed by Manchester's chief education officer, and may be replicated across the area. The main anxiety is that the funding available may not be sufficient for the diffusion of the scheme to be properly supported. See *Guardian* Education Supplement, 'Joined-up care', 27 May 2003.

26 see King M and Piper C, *How the Law thinks about Children*, 2nd edn (Aldershot: Gower, 1995).

27 for more information about these initiatives see Hocking G and Thomas G, *Other peoples children: why their quality of life is our concern* (London: Demos, 2003). Also the websites of the Regional Coordination unit www.rcu.gov.uk and the Children and Young People's Unit www.cypu.gov.uk give details of some of these policies and intitiatives.

28 see Chapman J, *System Failure: why governments must learn to think differently* (London: Demos, 2002), and Katz and Pinkerton,

Evaluating Family Support: thinking critically, thinking internationally (Chichester: Wiley, 2003 forthcoming).

29 Bateson G et al, *Steps to an Ecology of Mind: collected essays in anthropology, psychiatry, evolution and epistemology* (St Albans: Paladin, 2000).

30 Parton N, 'Risk, advanced liberalism and child welfare: the need to rediscover uncertainty, and ambiguity', *British Journal of Social Work* 28 (1998): 5–27.

31 Bronfenbrenner U, *The Ecology of Human Development: experiments by nature and design* (Cambridge, MA: Harvard University Press, 1979).

32 Chapman (2002) provides a number of examples of unintended consequences of targets and league tables, mainly in the health service.

33 Baginsky M, *Responsibility without Power? Local Education Authorities and child protection* (London: NSPCC, 2003).